Two Huerfano County Doughboys

Over there . . . somewhere in France

Doughboys: term for U.S. Infantry soldiers, first used in the Mexican-American War in 1846 but primarily associated with World War I. It may refer to soldiers' uniforms that were covered in chalky dust in the war in Mexico. *Time* Special Edition, World War I, The War That Shaped Our World, 2017.

Two Huerfano County Doughboys

Over there . . . somewhere in France The Epic Story Of Pvt. John A. Vigil and Pvt. Marcelo O. Reynolds And a few other Huerfanos In the Great War

Carl P. Lucero

Dedication

For those who have served, serving, and will serve—
For those who have made the supreme sacrifice— and will—
Lest we forget! The price of Freedom

Epigraphs

In great deeds, something abides. On great fields, something stays. Forms change and pass; bodies disappear; but spirits linger, to consecrate ground for the vision-place of souls. And reverent men and women from afar, and generations that know us not and that we know not of, heart-drawn to see where and by whom great things were suffered and done for them, shall come to this deathless field, ponder and dream; and lo! The shadow of a mighty presence shall wrap them in its bosom, and the power of the vision pass into their souls. This is the great reward of service. To live, far out and on, in the life of others; this is the mystery of the Christ, —to give life's best for such high sake that it should be found again unto life eternal[1]

— Major General Joshua L. Chamberlain, American Civil War

. . . you know, one of the things about losing any child — and you can't imagine until it happens, and I hope to God it never does for you or anyone — and it doesn't — it doesn't matter how they die…"And so, as a — as a person that's lost a — a child in combat — …when you lose one in combat, there's — there's a — in my opinion, there's a pride that goes with it, that he didn't have to be there doing what he was doing.

. . . He wanted to be there. He volunteered. Generally speaking, there's no encouragement in our society today to serve the nation, but many, many, many people do . . .

So I think they're special people, but they were doing what they wanted to do, and they were with who they wanted to be with, when they lost their lives. But I can tell you, it is the most — it caught me by surprise, the level of emotional impact . . .

. . . "Was it worth it?" "And I always go back with this: 'It doesn't matter. That's not our question to ask as parents. That person thought — that young person thought it was worth it, and that's the only opinion that counts.'

— Marine General John Kelly on the loss of his 29-year son killed in action, Afghanistan. Department of Defense Press Briefing in the Pentagon Briefing Room, January 8, 2016.

Contents

List of Illustrations

Preface

This story was prompted by an early twentieth-century photo of John Amado Vigil and Marcelo
Otto Reynolds. The photograph wasn't original, and its association with other Reynolds' family outdoor pictures
at first glance seemed like a hunting picture. A closer look, however, revealed that they were in military uniforms:
leggings and hats. The photo on the cover page must have been the original one, with copies for the families.

I found the picture engaging. Where were they wine tasting? Could the shape of the bottle reveal its content? When
and where was the photo taken? To which U.S. Army division were they assigned? In what campaigns did they
partake? The picture did not answer any of my questions, and when I asked— the answers I received were as grainy
as the picture, just somewhere in France.

I was working on replacing some of my father's World War Two (WWII) ribbons and medals, on giving him
a complete set, since someone misplaced them over the years. It became apparent that many of the places my
father's division fought were in the same general areas as the First World War. Henry "Red" Lucero, my father
(Marcelo's nephew) participated in the European Theatre: Northeast France, Netherlands, Belgium, Luxemburg,
and Germany. Henry was there from August 1944, through January 1946, with the 7th Armored Division, which
was assigned to the First, Second, and the Third U.S. Field Armies. All three armies had been activated in WWI,
1918, Northeast France.

Marcelo's resting place is at the Huerfano Masonic Cemetery, on the north end of Walsenburg, west of Main Street.
I had seen his marker many times, but it just had the inscription of "World War One," and that he was a "Private." I
didn't know where John Vigil was buried until viewing my great, great, Vigil grandparents' headstone. John Vigil's
upright headstone is in front of theirs, on the left side of the cemetery as you drive in from the main entrance, southwest of Marcelo's marker approximately ninety yards. On John's headstone is engraved, "John A. Vigil, Colorado,
Pvt., 110 Inf., 28 Div." From the sparse accounts I had heard over the years, I knew that they had served together in
the First World War, and John's headstone became a critical starting point.

After reviewing WWII records, I wondered if detailed unit history was documented on the WWI U.S. Army
Infantry Divisions. I accessed the internet and found the *History of the 110th Infantry, Pennsylvania* printed in
1920 which had been scanned. The 110th Infantry had recorded their journey from the United States to France,
their participation, and then back to the United States. Names of both John[2] "Amo" and Marcelo[3] were in it, as well
as a few other Huerfano County soldiers. However, Amo, Marcelo, and some of "The Forty and Four Braves"[4] did
not get assigned to the 28th National Guard Infantry Division until July 25th, 1918.[5] I thought I had everything
I needed with this book to capture their story. Other Huerfano recruits were along with Amo and Marcelo from

the day they left Huerfano County to their first engagement in the Second Battle of the Marne. Other Huerfanos mentioned in this book were included just due to their proximity to Amo and Marcelo's expedition.

Additional questions came about regarding their journey, such as, where were they in relation to other WWI historical personalities: Harry Truman, George Patton Jr., John MacArthur, Joyce Kilmer, Alan Seeger, World War I Medal of Honor recipients Alvin York, of the 82nd Infantry Division, and Charles Whittlesey, 308th Infantry, 77th Division, "Lost Battalion," (which was never lost). How did Humphrey Bogart get into this picture? At the time of writing their account, I did not come across any of Amo's or Marcelo's personal correspondence, other than what was published in the Walsenburg newspapers. The Y.M.C.A. would have the soldiers send home standard notes. Upon landing in Liverpool, the soldiers filled out cards letting their families know that they made to England safely. Many other soldiers who were on the same train with Amo and Marcelo kept records of their experiences such as Huerfano Louis B. Sporleder Jr., one of the Brave Forty-Four who wrote about their journey from Walsenburg to Camp Funston. A first lieutenant was on the same transport ship with them from New York to Liverpool and kept meticulous notes. Herbert Harmes from Gardner left four weeks before Amo and Marcelo, and his story was posted in *The Walsenburg World,* October 17th, 1918; Herbert spoke about his journey from New York harbor to Liverpool, then to Southampton, England, next to Château-Thierry, France. The Association of the 110th Infantry picks up their account written in the *History of 110th Infantry (10th Pa.) of the 28th Division.* Many of the dates, locations, miles marched, and casualties referenced in this story are from the History of the 110th Infantry, the 110th Association, "Abbreviated War Diary" pages 164-168. Amo and Marcelo are with the Second Battalion.

Perhaps in someone's garage or closet lies some worn out faded tear-stained letters that the Vigils or Reynolds may have stored. It has been a hundred years, and it is incredible how fast yesterday disappears. I took stories shared by some of Marcelo's family and grandchildren; accounts were some probable hand-to-hand combat and the time Marcelo got caught in a cellar behind enemy lines and his encounter with a mortally wounded German soldier.[6] Due to the detailed history of the 110th infantry division, I was able to corroborate those accounts with reasonable accuracy. The grainy photo became clear and focused, revealing a lot more information about the two young Huerfanos enjoying a moment. Since I started this project late, and time moved as fast as a Huerfano County jackrabbit, it limited my ability to follow up with the Vigils and the Reynolds. Tracking down family even with the internet was not as easy as one would think—taxes and death do have priority.

I am confident that I was able to determine where and when this picture was taken, along with the other photos of Marcelo. Though my goal was to retrace their steps and see what it revealed, this story is by no means a comprehensive account. They were valorous, vibrant young men, part of our family and Huerfano County's shared heritage, who answered our country's call and in so doing passed the torch of freedom to our parents' generation.

Some called it the "Big Adventure."[7] Some disdained the phrase and commented that when you are looking death in the face, it's not an adventure.[8]

Look out Europe, here comes the fighting farmers, ranchers, and a few miners from Huerfano County! Hopefully, this book reflects their story.

Acknowledgments

The following organizations and their volunteers helped make this book possible. First and foremost is the Huerfano County Historical Society, its volunteers, and the contribution from the Alton M. Tirey estate. It was through this organization that I was able to access the online *Walsenburg World* and hard copies of *The Independent* which John Van Keuren, a valiant volunteer, helped.

Many thanks to *The World Journal*: Huerfano, Las Animas, and Colfax counties, Publisher/Editor in Chief, Gretchen Sporleder Orr, and contributors such as Nancy Christofferson and Carolyn Newman. The Sporleders have contributed to the history of Huerfano County for over a hundred and forty years. Dorothy Rose Ree's book *Walsenburg-Crossroads Town* is a must-read for any Huerfano. Also, the Karen Mitchell team which has created the website the *Huerfano County Resources* with data on the county.

Other sources and volunteers were from the U.S. Army Center of Military History; The Library of Congress, Stars and Stripes: The American Soldiers' Newspaper of World War I, 1918 to 1919; Colorado Historic Newspapers Collection; Colorado Railroad Museum (Robert W. Richardson Railroad Library and Collections); The National WWI Museum and Memorial (Edward Jones Research Center); The Denver Library: Western History and Genealogy Department; Pitkin County Library; Basalt Regional Library; Ancestry: Genealogy, Family Trees and Family History Records; Google Earth; The Internet Archives; and Wikipedia.

Appreciation goes to Marcelo's grandchildren Darryl Cordova and Madelyn Cisneros-Sena who I reached out to multiple times. They shared family oral history that they had heard over the years which was similar in nature to what we had received. Men who fought in WWI came back home had to find work, support, and raise families; most put the war far behind them. It wasn't until later in life that Marcelo shared more intimate war accounts with Darryl Cordova.[9] Darryl was born, raised, served in the U.S. Army, and still resides in Huerfano County.

Author Edward Gutierrez wrote a book in 2014, *Doughboys on the Great War: How American Soldiers Viewed Their Military Experience,* his book was reviewed by Major Darrin Hass. Major Hass writes that Gutierrez argues "that many soldiers returned from the trenches expressing honor, pride, and value in their experience versus the traditional view that they were disillusioned with their wartime service. . .. After the war, many states gave their returning veterans basic surveys to fill out about their combat service. . .. According to the author the soldiers 'fought for honor, manhood, comrades, and adventure, but especially for duty.'"[10]

Finally, many thanks to family and friends whom in retrospect I could not have been able to bring this book to the public domain. My brother Michael who read the first draft; and Sandra Sharp who also reviewed it. Another contributor along the way was Woody Creek legend and movie script writer Steveo—said "you can edit forever and put more pictures."

Introduction

. . . the four winds of heaven were stirring up the great sea . . . great beasts were coming up from the sea, . . .

—Daniel 7:2 (New American Standard Bible)

The first two decades of the twentieth century were just the beginning of events that would confront the sensibilities of humanity throughout the world. This so-called first world war is estimated to have consumed nine to eleven million in just military lives,[11] and then the 1918-1919 influenza pandemic is estimated at fifty million people dead[12]— death reveled and reigned! This storm of pride taking root in the heart of Europe became known as World War One. Nations throughout the earth were in a state of unrest and some in revolutions. The West turned all its technological advances into killing its fellow man, from the heavens to the great seas like never before. The West mobilized approximately 49.6 million men into ". . . a monstrous massacre of human beings who prayed to the same God, loved the same joys of life, and no hatred of one another except as it had been lighted and inflamed by their governors . . ." wrote Sir Philip Gibbs.[13] Russia would commit 15.8 million men to the war, Germany 13.2 million men, the British Empire 8.4 million men, and the United States 4.3 million men.[14]

Why are the nations in an uproar asked the Psalmist:[15] Mexico's political instability and civil unrest spilled into southern borders of the United States. Germany was encouraging Mexico to take back Texas, Arizona, California, and enticing Japan to go to war with the United States. The Ottoman Empire was at the end of its 600-year reign and was nothing more than a facade of its formal self. The European empires surged to fill the void, North Africa and the Middle East were for the taking, evident by the Sykes-Picot Agreement, officially known as the Asia Minor Agreement, ratified on May 16, 1916.

Russia in 1917, a year that marked the end of its empire went down a road of internal revolution and made a treaty with Germany. By the time the United States declared war and sent troops in mid-1917, large numbers of Armenians had been systematically killed. The poem *In Flanders Fields,* where ". . . the poppies blow between crosses, row on row . . ." was already written in 1915. The Battle of Verdun was in 1916, which left the French military in a state of low morale. By mid-July of 1917, the European empires were bloodied, in a stalemate, and didn't know that their way of life would be entering a new era, the end of empires and the rise of nationalism.

Perhaps before the Americans could train, mobilize, and arrive in France, the Central Powers could end the war on their terms. In the spring of 1918, Germany started five offensive thrusts at the Western Front with fresh troops from the Eastern Front. By July of 1918, the German army was within fifty miles of Paris, hoping that the French military would move its forces to defend Paris. More American soldiers were arriving just in time, many who had never experienced combat and would pay with their entrusted lives.

Sometimes we think that the first two decades of the twentieth century were a kinder, gentler era, but the first eighteen years of Huerfano County and the world in which Amo and Marcelo were becoming men was unraveling, not only globally, but locally, and personally as well. Huerfano County in the early twentieth century was in a boom cycle. People from all over the world were in Huerfano County to work in the coal mines or to provide consumer services and products. When Amo and Marcelo were six years old, there were over thirty-two different languages spoken in the county. Huerfano County's economic prosperity attracted Hispanics from New Mexico and the San Luis Valley; English, Scottish, Italians, Greeks, and eastern Europeans in the new decade of promise. With economic growth came misunderstandings and mistrust, resulting in hostilities between the coal miners and the owners to the point where Huerfano County Sheriff Jeff Farr felt it was necessary to set up a machine gun in the courthouse.[16] In April 1914, Amo was nineteen and Marcelo eighteen years of age, when the tension between the mine owners and miners resulted in what became known as the Southern Colorado Coalfield War.

Figure 1. U.S. Regular Army comes to Huerfano County

One well-known incident occurred near Ludlow, a tent-city twenty-five miles south of Walsenburg, between the state militia and striking miners. Gunfire erupted, and fire consumed the camp; death came for children, women, and men. The Seventh street shootings occurred in Walsenburg following the Ludlow outburst and a young Mike Lenzini was killed by a stray bullet in front of the family business.[17] Eventually, the U.S. Army Regular troops were brought in to help diffuse the angst. This was the world to which young men of Huerfano County were exposed.

Most of the Huerfanos, who fought with the American Expedition Force (AEF) in the Great War, the Forgotten War, and called Pershing Crusaders were citizen-soldiers. The Regular Army called these men "fighting farmers." Amo, Marcelo, and forty-two other Huerfano County recruits would be called the "Forty and Four Braves,"[18] to distinguish them from the "Five," or the "Thirty-Nine," draftees in 1917, eventually assigned to the 164 Depot Brigade in Camp Funston, Ft. Riley, Kansas. Perhaps after a month or six weeks later, they were transferred to Camp Kearney, near San Diego, California. Camp Kearney was named after Stephen Watts Kearney, who at the age of fifty-two, in July 1846 led 2,500 troops down the Santa Fe Trail, where they all would see the Spanish Peaks rising to southwest from their position.[19] Then in June of 1918, via train crossed the continent, 2,500 miles, to Camp Merritt, New Jersey or Camp Mills, Long Island New York. How long they were there did not surface in the immediate research, or if they got into New York City. Early troops had an opportunity to go to New York, but by late June there was an urgency to get the soldiers to Europe. According to 1st Lieutenant Milton E. Brand's record of the 304th Motor Pool, they were there for about twenty days in Camp Mills before boarding the SS *Lapland*.[20]

Next came a 3,500-mile transatlantic voyage from New York to Liverpool, England becoming *overseas casuals*. Then on to Southampton, 200 miles south of Liverpool, via train to a Rest Camp, a misnomer. From there they took another transport to cross the English Channel, 120 miles, to the port of Le Havre, France. Then on to Paris via train, another 150 miles, destination, Chateâu-Thierry, where they became the *replacements*. They would march approximately twenty miles before their first engagement. Some would not ever fire a shot at or see the enemy when they make the supreme sacrifice. Most of the Forty and Four Braves would be in the Second Battle of the Marne, but never fight in the Meuse-Argonne and or in the Lorraine sector when the Armistice took effect. In the spring of 1919, the living would begin their odyssey back to Huerfano County. Those killed in action wouldn't be returned until the spring of 1922. This is their story, deeds of individual bravery, from Huerfano County to the Champagne region of France and their journey back to Huerfano County.

PART I

Over Here

Figure 2.Walsenburg 1913

*City of Walsenburg, Main Street, 1913, before the Great War; perhaps a photo taken
just before the Southern Colorado Coal wars, facing south.*

Denver Public Library, Digital Collections

★

CHAPTER 1

Consider the Years of Many Generations

Figure 3.Monulita Valdez-Vigil

Figure 4. Juan D. J. Vigil

Amo and Marcelo were born in Huerfano County in 1895, Amo in January, and Marcelo in September. They were first cousins and grandsons of Juan de Jesus Vigil and Monulita Valdez-Vigil. The Vigils had made the seventy-six-mile journey to Huerfano County in 1867 from Manassa, Colorado and settled on the south bank in the valley of the Cuchara River Tributary.[21]

Figure 5. The Vigils Homestead, Cucharas Valley, ca. 1867

This geographical region became known as North Veta or *En Norte Veta* as the Hispanics called it. Traditionally the area's east boundary has been about five miles west of Walsenburg to as far west as North Abeyta Creek and extending north to the upper Sand Arroyo.

Amo's father, Damacio Vigil Sr. was five years old when his parents moved to Huerfano County.[22] Becoming of age, he married Margarita Vigil-Vigil from San Luis, Colorado. Amo was the second born of eight children. His youngest brother Damacio Vigil Jr. would serve as the Huerfano County Clerk and Recorder for approximately a decade. His younger sister Rachel would marry Claud T. Swift, who also fought in World War One, Company F, 163rd Infantry, 41st Division (Sunset), and would serve as Huerfano County Sheriff for fourteen years.

Marcelo's mother, Manuelita Vigil-Reynolds, Damacio's younger sister, was born in 1874, in North Veta. At the age of twenty-two, she married a Texan from San Antonio, Joseph Otto Reynolds. Marcelo was the first born and had five younger brothers and sisters, all of whom attended school in Huerfano County.

Amo and Marcelo would be there for the deaths of their grandparents, first Juan D.J. Vigil in July of 1912, at the age of seventy-seven, and then their grandmother Monulita in April 1914, sixty-eight years of age. Both died in North Veta where they called home for over forty-five years. Damacio Vigil Sr. fifty-one, and Joe Reynolds, fifty-two, would now be the patriarchs of the family.

Then in the summer of June 28, 1914, fifty-year-old Archduke Ferdinand and his wife Sophie, forty-six, Duchess of Hohenberg were assassinated, leaving their three children orphans. The assassination triggered a series of responses that led to World War One (WWI). By the fall of 1914, the European empires were at war with each other, and the fast winds of pride blew over the Atlantic to the Western Hemisphere. A war that was supposed to last only six weeks turned out to be a stalemate bleeding into a third year with no end in sight. The United States had declared itself to be a neutral country, but Mexico's political instability and Germanys' insidious meddling enticing Mexico to reclaim Texas, New Mexico, and Arizona added to the tension between the countries.

The United States' neutrality was compromised since 1915; unknown to the general public munitions were being shipped to the allies via passenger ships, one of which was the British ocean liner RMS *Lusitania*. By the time President Wilson declared war in 1917, the United States was shipping food and other needs to the Allied Powers. Men from affluent and influential families were fighting and flying for the French. Former U.S. President Theodore Roosevelt's son, Quentin, was one of them. Alan Seeger, a Harvard graduate, was fighting for the French Legion and was killed in action on July 4, 1916, at the age of twenty-eight. He authored the well-known poem *I Have a Rendezvous with Death*, one of President John F. Kennedy's favorite poems.

The United States Regular army in 1917 was ranked 28th right behind Romania and unprepared for war. The *Independent* headlines read on April 6, 1917, "War Now On," 2,000,000 men wanted. General Pershing sent a cable to the War Department early in July to have a 1,000,000 man army in France by May 1918. Our standing army in the spring of 1917 was less than 135,000 men,[23] over 300,000 men if you included the National Guard.[24] In 1917, the Central Powers (Germany, Austria-Hungary, Ottoman Empire, and Bulgaria) had ten million men and the Allied Powers approximately eight million men.

Our military contribution was not taken seriously. By the time the U.S. would mobilize, train, and ship troops, perhaps the Central Powers could deliver a knockout. The Allies needed men and provisions, and the United States was abundant with both. But not to fear, *The Independent* carried the following article dated April 3, 1917. A noted seer, Prof. White wrote "No War with Germany and no Railroad Strike."

Prof. J.A. White of Denver, a psychological healer and seer, was here first of the week, arranging for a Walsenburg lecture date, a few weeks hence. Prof. White has gained a reputation in many sections of Colorado as a seer of ability. He predicted last fall that there would not then be a railroad strike. He was right. He predicts now that there will be no railroad strike. He predicts that there will be no war between the United States and Germany, but that war between this country and Japan will be declared in 1918, because of Mexico. Prof. White has promised to send to The Independent next week, the result of the Walsenburg municipal election, April 3rd.

CHAPTER 2

WAR NOW ON! Tall, Medium, or Short

"War Now On," is the headline on April 6th, of *The Independent*. Two million men wanted! In the spring of April 1917, the sons of Huerfano County were summoned, as well as the rest of the country, to enter the European fray. Amo was now twenty-two years old, a former college man, single, tall, good looking, and living and working for the Vigil enterprise in North Veta. Marcelo twenty-one, was ranching and farming with his parents in Tioga, and had an eye for young Sara Martinez from Badito. By April 13th the newspapers carried news of volunteers and urged young men not to wait for the "Selective Service," with headlines like "Patriots will not wait to be drafted." By Friday, May 11th, the country would soon be reaching out to ten million men. The Selective Act, a national draft passed on May 18th, required all men between the ages of 21 and 30 years old to register. Every man of military age was solely responsible for his registration, June 5th.

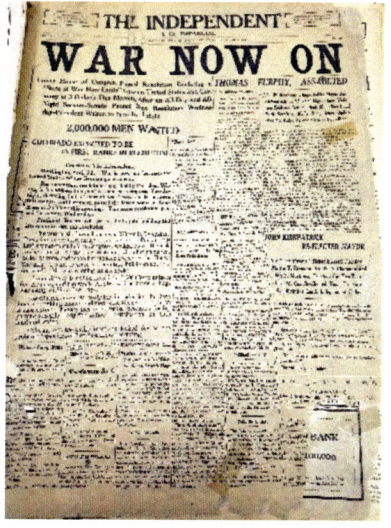

The front page of *The Independent* Friday, June 1st, stated in big bold letters, "A jail penalty awaits those who do not register Tuesday, June Fifth," Tuesday will be Registration Day. Registration day came, and over 1,539 men registered; there were no incidents that made the papers. Amo signed in at precinct 8, home address Cucharas and Marcelo at precinct 30, home address, Tioga. At the time both were single, no dependents, not bald, and had all their body parts; which were some of the fifteen questions. Amo a tall and Marcelo a medium.

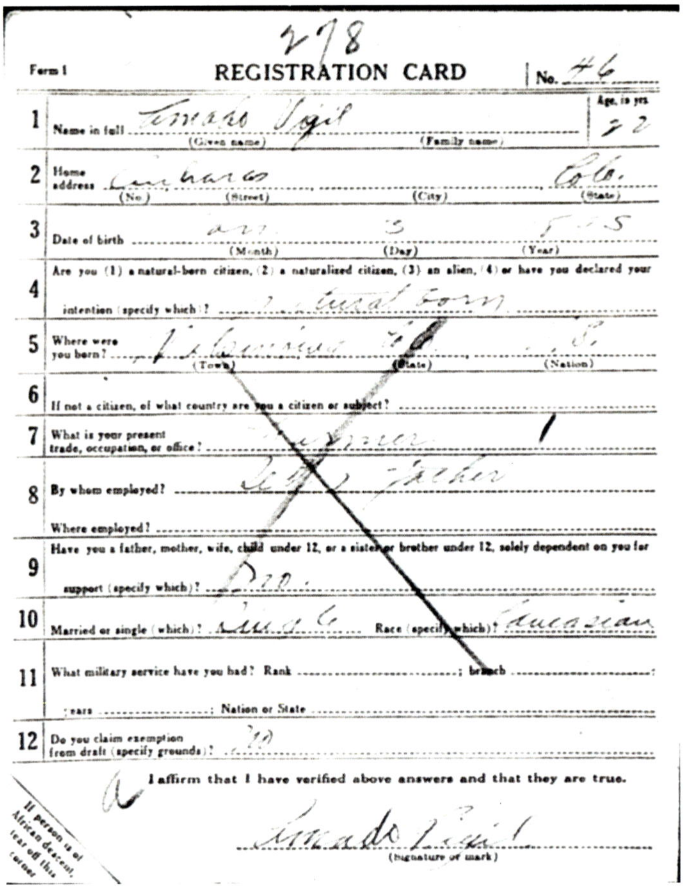
278

Form 1 REGISTRATION CARD No. 46

1 Name in full Amado Vigil (Given name) (Family name) Age, in yrs. 22

2 Home address (No.) (Street) (City) Colo. (State)

3 Date of birth (Month) (Day) (Year)

4 Are you (1) a natural-born citizen, (2) a naturalized citizen, (3) an alien, (4) or have you declared your intention (specify which)? Natural born

5 Where were you born? (Town) (State) (Nation)

6 If not a citizen, of what country are you a citizen or subject?

7 What is your present trade, occupation, or office? Farmer

8 By whom employed? Self, father

Where employed?

9 Have you a father, mother, wife, child under 12, or a sister or brother under 12, solely dependent on you for support (specify which)? No

10 Married or single (which)? Single Race (specify which)? Caucasian

11 What military service have you had? Rank ; branch ; years ; Nation or State

12 Do you claim exemption from draft (specify grounds)? No

I affirm that I have verified above answers and that they are true.

Amado Vigil (Signature or mark)

If person is of African descent, tear off this corner

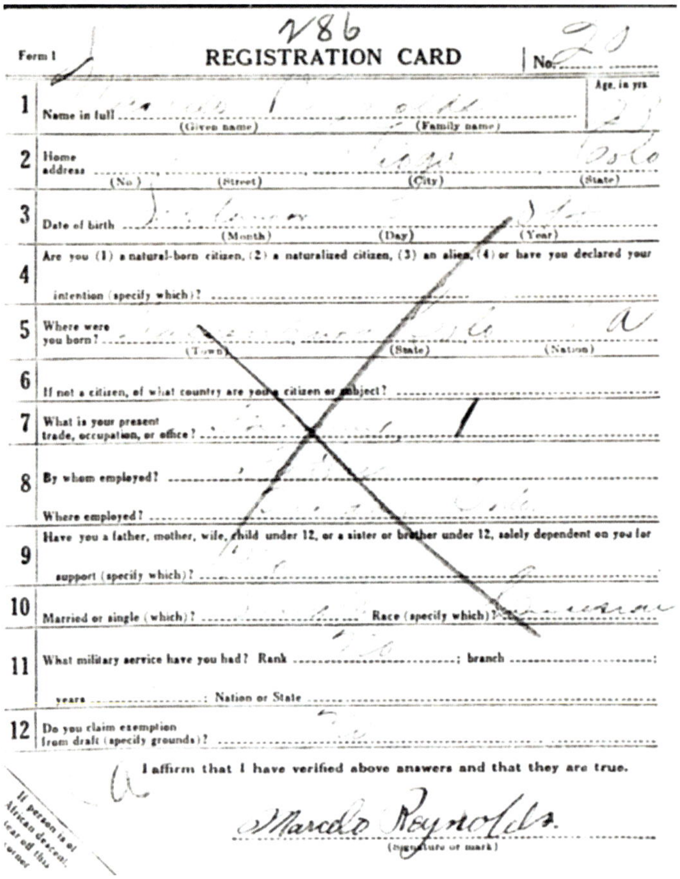
286

Form 1 REGISTRATION CARD No. 20

1 Name in full (Given name) (Family name) Age, in yrs.

2 Home address (No.) (Street) (City) Colo (State)

3 Date of birth (Month) (Day) (Year)

4 Are you (1) a natural-born citizen, (2) a naturalized citizen, (3) an alien, (4) or have you declared your intention (specify which)?

5 Where were you born? (Town) (State) (Nation)

6 If not a citizen, of what country are you a citizen or subject?

7 What is your present trade, occupation, or office?

8 By whom employed?

Where employed?

9 Have you a father, mother, wife, child under 12, or a sister or brother under 12, solely dependent on you for support (specify which)?

10 Married or single (which)? Race (specify which)? Caucasian

11 What military service have you had? Rank ; branch ; years ; Nation or State

12 Do you claim exemption from draft (specify grounds)?

I affirm that I have verified above answers and that they are true.

Marcelo Reynolds (Signature or mark)

If person is of African descent, tear off this corner

Figure 6. Amado Vigil and Marcelo Reynolds signed registration cards

CHAPTER 3

Extra Extra "FIRST CALL"

From the day that the Huerfanos registered, June 5th, to the first call was fifty-three days; each county in Colorado was to meet its quota, and Huerfano County's was ninety-eight. The front page of *The Independent*, "First Call," Thursday, August 2nd, listed over 200 names, with the first sixty-five to appear for examination from notice. Amo and Marcelo were not part of the first call.

Between registration and first call, Marcelo's father Joseph O. Reynolds, at the age of fifty-seven, died June 27th. He was a Huerfano County citizen for twenty-five years and operated a stock ranch at Badito; he was born in 1860, San Antonio, Texas. Most American families of the First World War soldier had neither seen nor experienced war. The last significant military engagement was the Civil War which had been over fifty-two years ago. Most were sons of ranchers, farmers, and miners. *The Independent*, on the front-page Friday, May 11th documents that over sixty Huerfanos volunteered, notably Ralph Levy, who was designated a captain. They became Troop F, First Colorado Cavalry. It seemed throughout Huerfano County most men were eager to join the cause and were encouraged by the local

"THE FIRST FIVE"

The above is a photograph of the first five Huerfano county young men, who went from here to Camp Funston, Fort Riley, Kansas, to form part of the new National army. They are, left to right: Charles Pierson, Floyd Babbitt, Samuel McCracken, Vincent Furphy and Edward Krier.

civic leaders of the day. The first to leave was Troop F, July 14th. After they encamp at Overland Park, Denver, then they are scheduled for California. They would be the first to go on the Denver & Rio Grande, 9:40 a.m. train; it was reported that practically every Huerfano resident came out to see them off. By August 17th, 206 had been examined, and 180 were to report to the county courthouse the following week. The second group to go was "The First Five": Charles Pierson, Floyd Babbitt, Edward Krier, "Fine"- Vincent Furphy, and Samuel McCracken who went to Camp Funston, Fort Riley, Kansas. Then on September 28th, came "the 39" who also went to Camp Funston.

Alfred A. Lovelace, who was part of the "39" wrote the following:

> All Kansas realizes now that Huerfano County, Colorado is "ON THE MAP," …" Tell the 'next bunch' that they now have a rep. to stick to," says Alfred T. Lovelace, captain of the thirty-nine," "Our boys were right on the dot, at every place. Had no trouble with them, and they were the life of the 600. "I have not been able to see 'the five boys from Huerfano County, send best regards.

Private Daniel Vigil, no relation to Amo Vigil, wrote to the Huerfano County Superintendent on September 29, regarding his experience en route to Camp Funston. His letter printed in *The Independent*, front page, Friday, October 5, 1917.

> …I feel proud to say that the boys from Walsenburg were the merriest "bunch" on train, from departure to arrival. Wherever the train stopped, and we had an opportunity, we formed parades, march, sang and cheered for "Old Glory," and Huerfano county. We had a large "Red-White and Blue" displayed in our coach which we all cheerfully contributed to purchase.

The next bunch are called "the Forty and Four Braves," and one of them was a newlywed. Marcelo and Sara Martinez-Reynolds were married on September 19th, in North Veta just nine days earlier. This was the third contingent of the quota of ninety-eight. They were notified, on September 28th, to report to the courthouse Tuesday morning, October 2nd, and be prepared to leave Wednesday morning October 3rd, on the 9:40 a.m. train. It was Amo and Marcelo's turn; they would take the same route as the "First Five" and "the 39" to Camp Funston.

Huerfano County once again rose to the occasion of sending off the Forty and Four Braves, and *The Independent* wrote that nearly 1,000 people assembled at the Star Theatre Tuesday night to bid farewell to the men and the newlywed. The newspaper wrote that they prayed, sang, and spent time with the Huerfano County recruits. The stage was decorated with three large American flags and smaller

Camp Funston, Kansas, Was Enriched, Yesterday, by the Addition of our Largest National Army Quota---Over 1,000 People at Depot When "Soldier Special" Left to Wave Farewell to Boys---Thomas Sullivan, Captain and William E. Thomas, Assistant, enroute

"THE FORTY AND FOUR BRAVES"

Thomas Sullivan, Captain	William Bodycomb	Marcelo Raynolds
William E. Thomas, Asst. Capt.	Epimenio Hurtado	Duvigen Leyba
George J. Spraitzer	John Bione	Andy Martinez
Anastacio Trujillo	Rufus P. Harriman	Gaspar Martinez
Antonio Andreakis	Louis B. Sporleder, Jr.	Blas Gutierrez
William T. Fall	John S. Chavez	Michael Gallini
Luis A. Sons	Abran Arguello	John Olsafsky
Delfino Gallegos	William Snedden	Guillermo Garcia
John Coan	David Price	John Stack
Amado Vigil	Albert Matteroli	John B. Bertolero
Marcelo Trujillo	Joseph Skinsky	Leon Poli
Cecilio Orado	Samuel Gonzalez	Candido Lucero
Steve Mancoff	Donaciano Montoya	William H. Sears
Orio McRae	Mike H. Duzenack	Alexander Osvik
	Eusebio Martinez	Abenicio Velasquez

Forty-four more of our National army quota of selected soldiers left Walsenburg at 9:35 o'clock last Wednesay morning, for Fort Funston, Kansas.

Figure 7. The Forty and Four Brave

ally-flags, an orchestra, and a program that lasted over an hour and a half. Louis B. Sporleder Jr. sang one of his solos. After the program they spent another hour smoking, conversing, and bidding farewell to friends. Louis B. Sporleder Jr. was appointed "official news reporter."

CHAPTER 4

We're Coming Lafayette

The waiting was over for the third group. "The Forty and Four Braves" reported to the Walsenburg train depot to board the 9:40 a.m. train #110-10, Denver & Rio Grande-Western Pacific, the Pueblo & Denver Express.[25] On Wednesday, October 3rd, over a thousand Huerfanos were gathered to wish the brave God's speed. The #110 iron horse came in with its steam-powered whistle, as it brought its Pullman coaches. The "Soldier's Special" as they called it was ready to take their sons away on the first leg of their great adventure. All boarded except one, and a steely eye undersheriff spied him in a buggy. He was arrested, taken to the county jail, and charged for being "a slacker!"

One can assume that some of the young men to say good-bye, who were of age and registered on June 5th, were Amo's older brother, twenty-six-year-old Alfredo, and Marcelo's brother-in-law, twenty-five-year-old Porfirio Lucero. Both were married with dependents and employed, so, for now, they were exempt. Producing food and coal would be critical to the war effort, and they were actively working. Draft boards classified men into five groups: eligible, deferred, exempted but available, exempted due to hardship, and ineligible.[26]

The whistle blew and the DR&GWP #110 steamed on to Pueblo, arriving at 11:50 a.m., and then left at 12:30 p.m., arriving in Denver Union Station at 4:30 p.m., 168 miles in six hours. There the Huerfano County brave entrained the #104 Union Pacific, Kansas City Express eastbound for Junction City, Kansas, departing around 8:30 p.m. With five hundred miles in front of them they would wake up in Fort Riley, in the State of Kansas.

Figure 8. Pueblo Union Deport, 1910

Photographs by George L. Bean

Denver Union Station 1913

Amo, Marcelo, and the other Forty and Two Braves arrived in Camp Funston, Thursday afternoon, October 4th, close to a 700-mile trip in over twenty-two hours. L. B. Sporleder Jr. the appointed "official news reporter," wrote to *The Independent* and it was posted on the October 12, 1917, front page:

We, the forty-four soldiers of the last contingent of Huerfano County, wish to express our hearty thanks to the people of Walsenburg and Huerfano County for their generous reception given in honor of our departure for the training camp. Throughout the entire journey, our boys were in the best of spirits and upheld the good name of Huerfano County.

Upon our arrival in Pueblo, we were escorted to the depot dining room, where we partook of a fine dinner. While in the station, the Pueblo quota arrived and from there on to Denver we picked different quotas from each County, making in all five coaches.

We arrived in Denver about 4:30, were taken to the Y.M.C.A. in large sight-seeing cars, had a swim and later took in "sights of the city." At 6 o'clock a dinner, given under the auspices of the Denver Red Cross was served us in the union station. Because of the Huerfano County boys showing an unusual cheerful nature, we were called on three times by Governor Gunter, who gave us all the best of good wishes. At 8:30 three sections were due to leave Denver, ours being the first section of ten Pullmans.

We arrived in camp Funston Thursday afternoon, were taken to our barracks where we made our own mattresses out of hay and received one blanket each. The nights are quite cold, so now the boys are doubling up, until we receive more bedding. As yet, we have not received our uniforms, but are wearing union overalls. Over 19,000 soldiers arrived here last week. We again wish to thank the people of Huerfano County for their many kindnesses.

DENVER, COLORADO SPRINGS, PUEBLO, WALSENBURG AND TRINIDAD

	READ DOWN						READ UP	
	15-115 Colorado-New Mex. Express	5-109 Trinidad and Walsenburg	Miles	Table No. 8 STATIONS	Elevation	110-10 Pueblo & Denver Express	116-16 Colorado New Mex. Express	
......	* 7.30 pm	* 9.15 am	0.0	Lv ....DENVER......Ar	5280	* 4.30 pm	* 7.30 am	......
......	10.20 pm	12.02 pm	74.9	Lv..COLORADO SPRINGS..Ar	5989	1.50 pm	4.30 am	......
......	11.30 pm	1.15 pm	119.4	Ar.....PUEBLO.....Lv	4668	12.30 pm	3.05 am	......
......	12.10 am	1.30 pm	119.4	Lv......PUEBLO......Ar	4668	11.50 am	2.45 am	......
......	12.25 am	1.45 pm	122.9	Ar SOUTHERN JUNCTION.Lv	4822	11.35 am	2.25 am	......
......	f 12.45 am	f 2.06 pm	134.0	Ar.......Marnel.......Lv	5130	f11.12 am	f 1.45 am	......
......	f 1.02 am	f 2.23 pm	142.7	Ar....Cedarwood.....Lv	5606	f10.53 am	f 1.30 am	......
......		2.44 pm	156.7	Ar......Huerfano.....Lv	5677	10.29 am		......
......		3.10 pm	168.7	Ar CUCHARA JUNCTION.Lv	5942	10.10 am		......
......	2.00 am	3.25 pm	175.2	Ar....Walsenburg.....Lv	6187	9.45 am	12.35 am	......
......		3.30 pm	168.7	Lv....Walsenburg......Ar	6187	9.40 am		......
......		4.08 pm	177.6	Ar.ROUSE JUNCTION.Lv	6148	9.06 am		......
......		4.43 pm	194.5	Ar.......Barnes.......Lv	6232	8.35 am		......
......		f 4.51 pm	198.3	Ar...Chicosa Junction...Lv	6116	f 8.27 am		......
......		5.08 pm	206.0	Ar....El Moro.......Lv	5879	8.10 am		......
......		5.20 pm	210.3	Ar....TRINIDAD....Lv	5994	8.00 am		......

* Daily.   † Daily except Sunday.   f Stops on flag.
‡ On Saturdays and Sundays No. 29 leaves Denver at 6.00 p.m.
x Monday, Wednesday and Friday.   y Tuesday, Thursday and Saturday.
z Tuesday only.   ¶ Runs via Walsenburg Junction.

19

Figure 9. Denver and Rio Grande-Western Pacific 1917 Schedule

Colorado Railroad Museum, Robert W. Richardson Railroad Library and Collections

Another group of 200 men came in the day before on October 3rd, 11:00 a.m., they were assigned to the newly formed 314th Motor Supply Train, and 1st Lieutenant Milton E. Bernet wrote the following:

Thousands were already streaming into Funston…huge special trains rolled into the station which bore the name of the County from which the occupants came and such legends as "From Osage County to Berlin," or "Can the Kaiser," the men were hurriedly run through a receiving station, separated by counties, and assigned to the various infantry and artillery regiments, the engineer regiment, the field signal and machine gun battalions, and the trains.[27]

Figure 10. Denver Union Station ca. 1913

Camp Funston located near Junction City, Kansas, was the largest of 16 divisional cantonment training camps built in World War One. The camp was named for Brigadier General Frederick Funston, known as "Fighting Fred." Camp Funston was laid out in city block squares with main streets and side streets. The camp resembled a city, with general stores, theaters, social centers, infirmaries, libraries, schools, workshops, and a coffee roasting house. The sleeping barracks were 43 feet by 140 feet and two stories high. Each had a kitchen, mess hall, company commander's office, supply rooms, and squad rooms or dormitories. There were 150 beds in each sleeping room, as that was the size of an infantry company in 1917. An estimated 2,800 to 4,000 buildings were on 2,000 acres; present-day Walsenburg is 1,913 acres.

A letter was written from Edward Krier who with the "Big Five," ". . . the barracks are 150 feet long by 42 feet wide or 6,300 square feet, two stories high, including a mess room, supply room and sleeping quarters. The room is almost all windows with plenty of light and good air, able to house 200 men. Lights are turned off at 9:30 p.m. and they got up at 6:00 a.m.," Krier states that it has been so cold no one could sleep and wrote the following:

. . . each was issued a hat, two pairs of shoes, three suits of underwear, five pairs of sox, gloves, overalls, and jumpers. Each had cots with two blankets, and the entire camp is filled with the boys in blue. The government allowed 40 cents per day, per man, for food. We wash our own dishes and have learned to do it by using dirt on and washing with cold water, although there is a tub of hot soapy water to do it in; but, as everyone uses this same tub it gets greasy . . . .

Vincent Furphy, of the Big Five wrote "Today is Saturday, and we are all off until Monday. We can go anyplace we want to. All of the officers are fine fellows. Trainloads arrive every day. All the houses are lighted and have steam heat. A good bunch of fellows where we stay. Everything just fine." Sam McCracken, of The Big Five, sent news back home to "Tell all the boys it is not bad."

Some of the things that the Big Five failed to mention after their twenty-two-hour journey, were that they had to discard their civilian clothes and take a cold shower. All the men were lined up and were sent one at a time for their shower. Breakfast was bacon, bread, and coffee.

Most of the camps had the same schedule of training: waking at first light to the notes of "Kahki Bill," which was also known as "Number Nine"; bayonet and physical training, bayonet work in the trenches, and going through wire entanglements; and rifle care. The time was filled with lectures, singing, military courtesy, uniform regulations, instruction regarding saluting, proper wearing of canteens, haversacks, first-aid pouches, guard duty, making packs, pitching shelter tents, patrolling, and parading. I wonder if singer Louis B. Sporleder Jr. became an instructor, he was already designated a sergeant when he came home on furlough in May 1918.

Most of the Huerfanos were assigned to an infantry depot company, which Edward Krier, one of the Big Five, explained "is one where other brigades come for men needed to fill up."

There are letters written from some of the men from Huerfano, but very few notes on their being on leave. Manuelita, Marcelo's mother commented in *The Independent*, dated August 30th, 1918, that she had not seen Marcelo since he left October 1917.

At some point, Amo, Marcelo, and other Huerfanos left Camp Funston for Camp Kearny, San Diego. The winter of 1917 turned out to be one of the coldest in our nation's history, which could have been one of the main reasons why they were transferred to Camp Kearny, a train ride of approximately 1,600 miles. Herbert Harmes from Gardner states in his account to a gathering in Walsenburg that after a month in Camp Funston he left for Camp Kearny. Anastacio Trujillo's obituary, revealed that he was in Camp Kearny with other Walsenburg men. On the SS *Lapland*'s ship manifest, it states: "Camp Kearny June Automatic Replacements."

The Huerfanos troop train from Camp Kearny may have returned to Camp Funston and picked up the 304th Motor Supply Train and shared that portion of the trip with the 304th. In June 1918, they arrived either in Camp Merritt, New Jersey or Camp Mills, Long Island New York, another 2,900 miles, well over forty hours of travel. They boarded the same ship as 1st Lieutenant Milton E. Bernet and the 304th on June 28th. By the time some of the forty-four braves embark overseas they may have traveled well over 5,200 miles via rail, known as the coffee, cookie, and cigarette express. They may have seen the Pacific Ocean, parts of Mexico, and traveled coast to coast through twelve states all in their early twenties. The Huerfanos would now be prepared to travel overseas on a coal-fired, steam-powered transport ship, nonstop to Liverpool, England, the old country and then more trains.

CHAPTER 5

Back to the Old World

On Thursday, June 27th, 12:15 p.m., embarkation began for some of "the forty and four braves," the same day Marcelo's father had died one year ago. When Amo and Marcelo looked over the deck perhaps there was a moment of remembrance for Joe Reynolds. They boarded the SS *Lapland* in the port of New York, Pier 61, N. R., destination Liverpool, England. The SS *Lapland* was a 1908 Belgian Red Star 18,565-ton steam-powered passenger ship converted in June of 1917, to a troop transport ship, 603 feet long, a 72-foot beam and a speed of 17 knots. Instead of her former distinctive sleek colors, the SS *Lapland* was repainted gray and white to camouflage it on the high seas.

Red Star Line
New
Twin-Screw
Steamer
"Lapland"

Figure 11. SS Lapland

They finished boarding at 2:40 p.m., some of the forty-four brave in addition to Amo and Marcelo were Mauricio Trujillo from Clover; Lute Cordova, Walsen; Moses Benavidez and Anastacio Trujillo, from Rouse; John Chavez, Duvigen Leyba, Guillermo Garcia, of Gardner; and William Snedden, of La Veta. Although he was not part of Huerfano group, Ruben Vigil who was from Trinidad. Men from nearby cities represented on the ship were from Pueblo, Raton, and Denver. They were classified as "Camp Kearny, June Automatic Replacements, Draft: Five Companies of casuals #11; #12; #13; 14; and #15; a total of 1,248, composed of officers, above grade, and below grade. Amo and Marcelo plus some of the other Huerfanos were most likely part of the 13th Co., Overseas Casuals.

The ship was designed to accommodate 1,500 passengers, but it was loaded with 2,226 men and women. On the ship with the Huerfanos were Signal Corps Telephone operators, Unit #4- Female; the 314th Motor Supply Train, composed of 522 men assigned to the 89th U.S. Army Division; Base Hospital personnel; and 50 casual officers who for the most part were railroad engineers. In addition to troops, a group of Japanese statesmen and a number of English officers and their wives were also on board.

Their voyage would take them near the vicinity of three maritime tragedies where many had traveled before. Two were well-known, and the third was in the shadows of the past. The three were the RMS *Titanic,* which sank in 1912, when it struck an iceberg; the second, the *RMS Lusitania,* which occurred three years earlier, torpedoed by a German submarine in May 1915, and the SS *Ville du Havre* which collided with another ship at two o'clock in the morning, 1873, and sunk in twelve minutes.

Horatio Spafford, a successful Chicago lawyer, lost four daughters to the SS *Ville du Havre* tragic sinking. It was probably pointed out to General Pershing where the SS *Ville du Havre* incident occurred that caused Horatio Spafford to pen the song it is *Well with my Soul.* Unexpectedly two years earlier, August 1915, General Pershing lost his wife and three daughters, ages six, seven, and eight to a severe house fire in San Francisco on the Presidio.

On Friday— a day sailors considered bad luck, June 28ᵗʰ, the same day Archduke Franz Ferdinand and his wife Sophie were assassinated four years earlier. Amo, Marcelo, and the other Huerfanos departed at 9:35 a.m. and were on the next stage of their big adventure. Fortunately for the men and women on the SS *Lapland,* they were allowed to be above deck. First Lieutenant Milton E. Bernet, with the 89th Division, wrote the following on leaving New York harbor.

Probably no one who was aboard the "Lapland" as it steamed away from New York harbor that early morning of June 28th, 1918, will ever forget the wonderful sight he [the troops] saw, the huge painted ships going out to sea, the thousands of soldiers some of whom were seeing their native land for the last time that morning. The War Department had but a few weeks before rescinded the regulation which previously had required all soldiers to remain below deck as the convoys left New York harbor.

They were determined earnest soldiers as they stood there, realizing the solemnity of that moment. The wonderful skyline of New York and the Statue of Liberty fading in the distance symbolized for them the greatness of the country which now had considered them sufficiently trained and ready to represent it in the greatest war of History, the struggle for civilization itself.

Regulations forbade the soldiers cheering, but the huge liners lying in the harbor could not be denied. As the great camouflaged ships left their moorings and plowed proudly out, they began a din of whistling which did not end until the ships had passed over the horizon.[28]

Many troops talked about the first time seeing and being on the sea. Private Herbert Harmes from Gardner who left the last day of May from New York did not mention leaving the harbor but went on to say "As soon as we reached the boat each man was given a life preserver that looks like a tire for an auto. This was kept around our waists . . . we did not remove our clothes or life preservers. We had no trouble on the way over"[29] Corp. Chester E. Baker in his diary wrote: "Every day of our crossing was bright and sunny and khaki-clad soldiers stood thick at the rails all through the voyage."[30]

Assembled by buglers, Amo, Marcelo, and the other Huerfanos had boat drills twice a day at 10:00 a.m. and 3:00 p.m. The second day out to sea, 1st Lt. Bernet wrote that many men were seasick and were so sick many could not make to the boat drills. Seven days into their voyage was the Fourth of July, where the men were mustered to see the raising of the American flag while the buglers blew "To the Colors." At eleven o'clock in the morning, there was a 21-gun salute given by the naval convoy, they listened to some speeches (one by the President of Cornell University), and fruits and candy were distributed. As the sun was setting, 1st Lt. Bernet said that the flag was lowered with the troops again in formation of boat muster.

During the last two or three days of the voyage, they were in the most dangerous part of their journey, the enemy submarine zone, and every precaution taken. Garbage, cigarette butts, paper, etc., were not allowed to be thrown overboard during the daytime but collected in cans and dumped into the sea at night. No one was permitted to smoke on deck after sundown, all port-holes were closed, and every person slept with his clothes on, with life preservers close at hand.

The SS *Lapland* convoy took the northerly route where 1st Lt. Bernet said the nights were almost as bright as the day. When well into the "danger zone," the convoy was met by a large number of destroyers. They made their way through the coasts of Scotland and Northern Ireland, separated by thirteen miles between them, where five months earlier on February 5, 1918, a German submarine, UB-77, torpedoed and sank the SS *Tuscania* troop transport ship with over 2,000 U.S. soldiers (approximately 200 would die). Nothing is mentioned of SS *Tuscania*, but the captain of the SS *Lapland* sure knew about it and still had another 180 miles to go. On the 9th of July the lights were flashed on the ship before midnight. This signal let them know that Liverpool was close, and they were safe. 1st Lt. Bernet wrote the following comments on the final days of the voyage:

Although the passage had been ideal, but little rain and no storm, there was probably no one on the boat who regretted its conclusion...Those days of looking out over the broad expanse of the sea were long ones, and in addition, the men were neither accustomed to the English ration nor again to the English ship's cooks.[31]

Two people died on the ship; one deceased person was buried at sea and another a soldier died while they were in the harbor at Liverpool. The next day the tide allowed the SS *Lapland* to dock and the troops were issued travel rations for their train ride.

Figure 12. Knotty Ash Depot near Liverpool, England

81st Division boarding a train en route for Southampton, August 14, 1918

Imperial War Museum [Great Britain]

Mr. and Mrs. Damacio Vigil have received word from their son who has arrived safely in Liverpool England, and will soon cross the canal to somewhere in France.

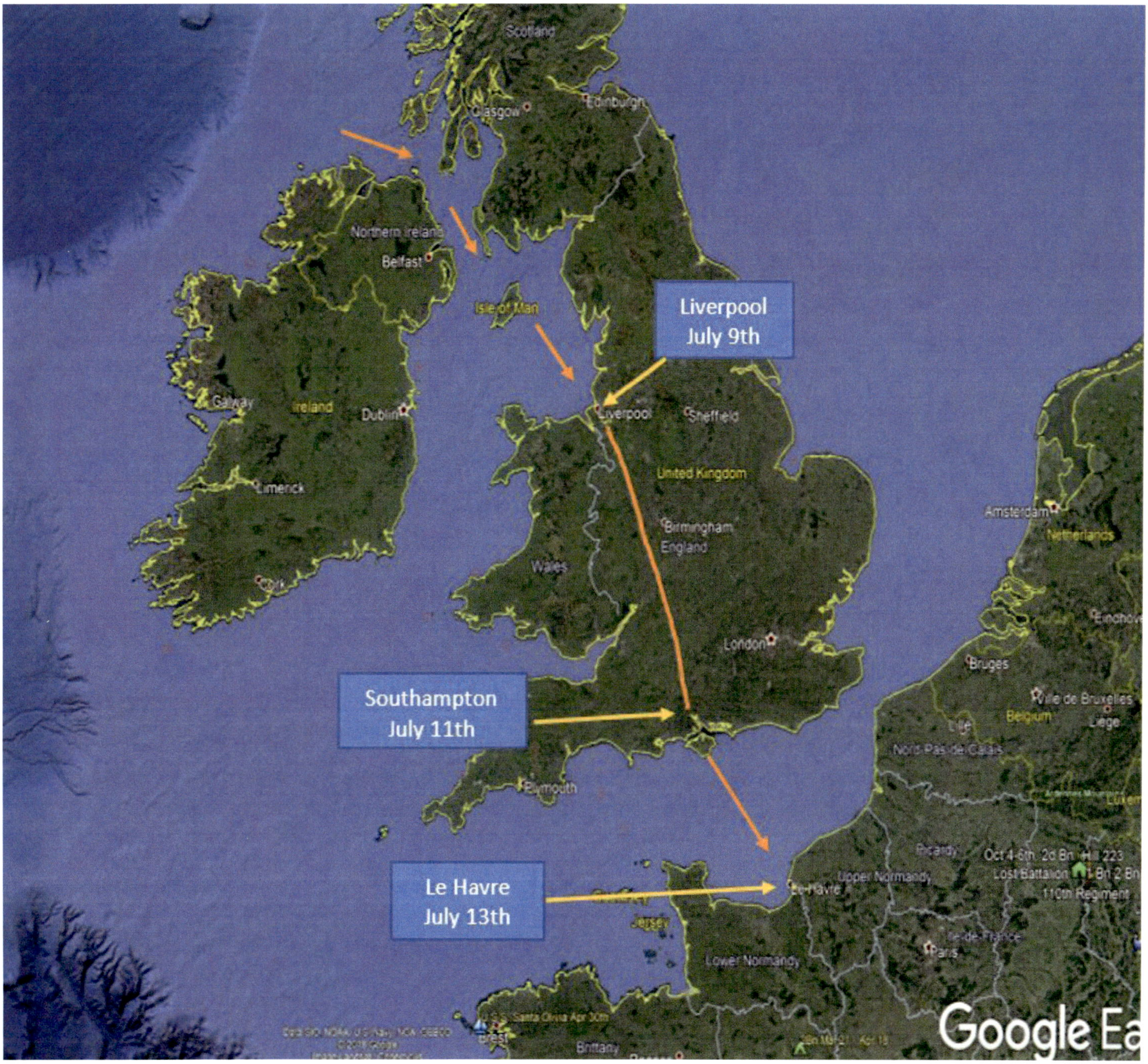

Figure 13. The Huerfanos en route to France

CHAPTER 6

Camp Disagreeable

As the SS *Lapland* was docking at 10:30 a.m., the residents of Liverpool, not be outdone by the citizens of Huerfano County, made it a memorable moment with a robust spirited greeting. The buildings were decorated with American flags and the British band played the Star-Spangled Banner. Upon debarkation, they were immediately separated by the Railway Transport officer, and marched from the docks to the Grand Central Terminal and entrained for Dover or Southampton, England. An Iowa Doughboy Private George Herring who landed in Liverpool about five days earlier before the Huerfanos commented they were "boarded on 'British toy trains,' for the port of Southampton. There they were 'packed like sardines,' into sometimes shabby channel boats and sailed to Le Havre, France."[32]

At this juncture, the Huerfanos could have gone either direction. If Southampton, they would land in Le Havre France. If Dover, then to Calais, France. For several reasons, it is likely that most of the Huerfanos went to Southampton, then crossed the English Channel to Le Havre. First, Herbert Harmes informed his Walsenburg audience in October 1918 that he was in a rest camp in Southampton; he had sailed about four weeks before Amo and Marcelo. Second, the German Spring Offensive may have strained the British positions in the Calais area. Subsequently, we lose track of Amo, Marcelo, and the other Huerfanos until they are assigned to the 28th U.S. Army Infantry Division in Chateâu-Thierry sector, the 25th of July.

There were accounts at the rest camps that they were kept there just long enough to discard their extra clothing and equipment, which had been so carefully issued before leaving the United States. "Rest Camp" was a misnomer.[33] It should have been called "Camp Disagreeable." While in camp they were introduced to English tea and jam, issued British gas masks, and listened to British sergeants lecture on the horrors of gas.

The doughboys who arrived in the middle of June of 1918, were swiftly assigned and prepared for the front lines versus the troops who came in April and May and had more time to train and acclimate. With the beginning of the end of the almost two-hundred-year Russian Empire in early 1917 and its treaty with Germany in March 1918, the German army was able to focus on the Western Front. In the spring of 1918, Germany anticipated delivering the final knockout blow to the Allies before the United States Army could be effectual. On December 31, 1917, the AEF strength was at 174,884, of which only the 1st Division had served at the front. Germany was bringing in large numbers, about fifty-divisions (a European division was about 15,000 troops) of trained and experienced troops from the Eastern Front.

PART II

We are here Lafayette

Figure 14. Doughboys entering Château-Thierry, July 1918

Library of Congress Prints and Photographs Division

★

CHAPTER 7

The Land of the Crushed Grape

Amo, Marcelo, and the other Huerfanos set foot in France around 13th of July, most likely at the Le Havre port. They would entrain on a French military train, which made the American ones seem luxurious compared to the French boxcars covered with straw. The train would take them toward Paris on a secondary railroad route to an area near Juilly, twenty miles northeast of Paris. Near Juilly they detrained, marched, and were carried on lorries to the Chateâu-Thierry sector.

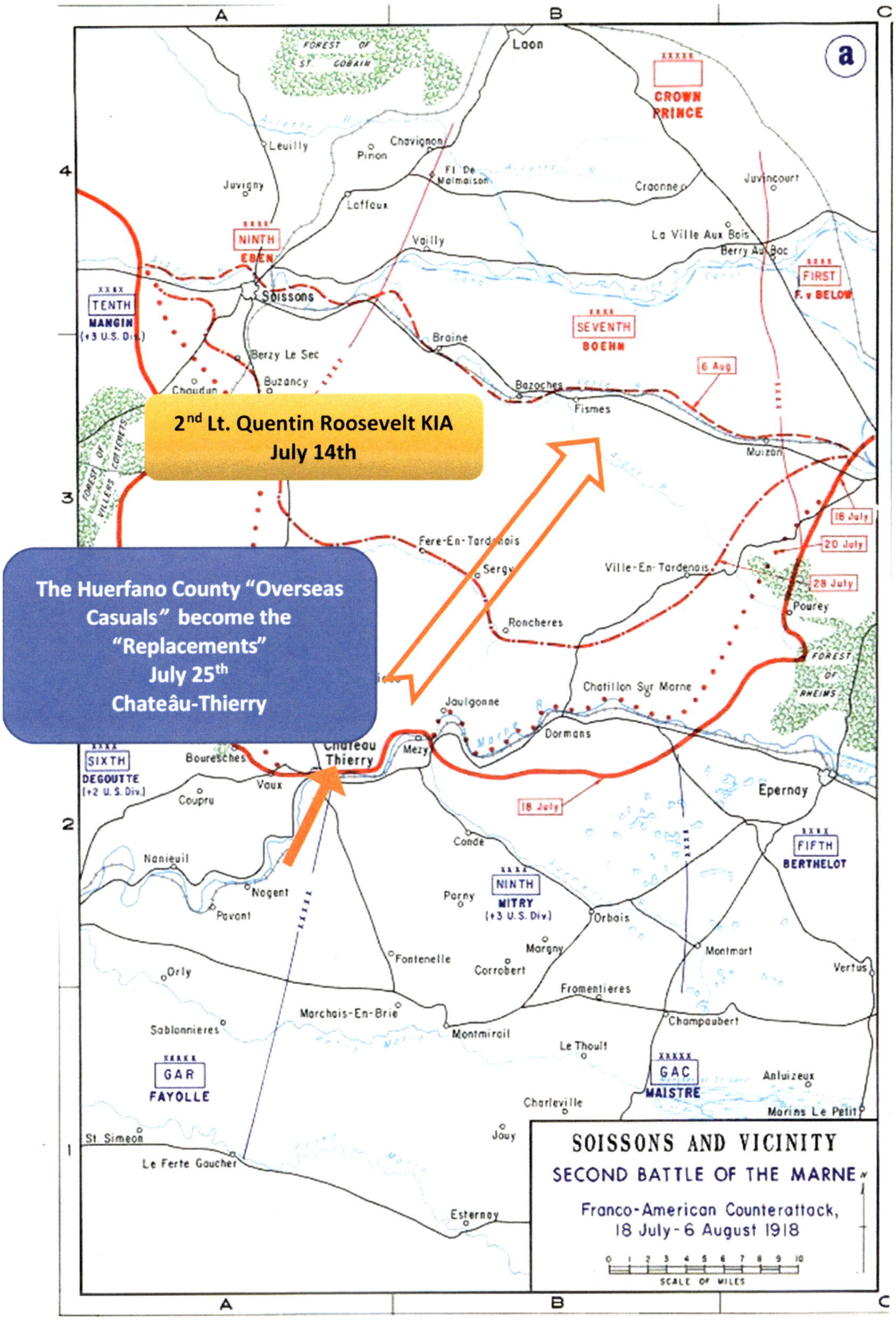

**2nd Lt. Quentin Roosevelt KIA
July 14th**

**The Huerfano County "Overseas Casuals" become the "Replacements"
July 25th
Chateâu-Thierry**

SOISSONS AND VICINITY

SECOND BATTLE OF THE MARNE

Franco-American Counterattack,
18 July - 6 August 1918

0 1 2 3 4 5 6 7 8 9 10
SCALE OF MILES

Figure 15. The Huerfanos in the Second Battle of the Marne

While the Huerfanos were in en route to Chateâu-Thierry, on a sweltering day, the 14th of July, Bastille Day, former President Theodore Roosevelt's twenty-year-old son Quentin was killed in action, shot down fourteen miles northeast of Chateâu-Thierry in the small village of Chamery.

The 28th Division National Guard (NG) records show that on Thursday, July 25th, over 400 replacements arrived. [34] The 28th Division was composed of three brigades: the 55th, the 56th, and the 53rd Field Artillery Brigade or approximately 28,000 troops at full strength including Divisional Troops and Trains. The elements of the 55th Infantry Brigade were the 109th Infantry, 110th Infantry, and the 108th Machine Gun Battalion (MGB). The 56th Infantry Brigade was composed of the 111th, 112th, and 109th MGB. The 53rd Field Artillery Brigade was made up of the 107th, 108th, 109th, and 103rd Trench Mortar Battery.

It is on July 25th, that some of the Huerfanos are assigned to the 110th Infantry Regiment, 55th Brigade. The 110th was composed of 3,000 men, three battalions of 1,000 men per battalion. Each battalion had four companies, with 250 troops per company. The First Battalion: companies A, B, C, and D. The Second Battalion: companies E, F, G, and H, and the Third Battalion: companies I, K, L, and M. Assigned to the Second Battalion: Amo,[35] Marcelo,[36] and Lute[37] to Company F; Moses[38] to Company H, and Ruben Vigil[39] of Trinidad to Company G. First Battalion: Maurico Trujillo[40] from Clover to Company D. Assigned to the Third Battalion: Dewgen Leyba[41] of Gardner to Company M.

The 25th of July finds the 110th Regiment bivouacked at La Canairdèrie Farm, three miles north of Charly-sur-Marne, seven miles upriver, southeast of Chateâu Thierry. The French military made the following comment: "An interesting point is that this division was made up of a great many men of German origin, who in thus shedding their blood for the United States gloriously showed their loyalty."[42] No doubt when the Huerfanos mentioned they were from Walsenburg; the Pennsylvanians must have recognized the German influence. The United States was approximately 60 percent "British" and 35 percent "German" in 1860 it had been transformed by twenty million immigrants who'd arrived in two decades before 1914.[43]

Ten days before the Huerfanos arrived, the 28th Division was in second position under the tactical orders of the fifty-two-year-old Brigadier French General Jean Joseph Degoutte of the French Sixth Army. They were near Conde Brie in the Chateâu-Thierry sector when the last German offensive took place. Two companies, B, and C of the 110th Regiment were mauled in the last German offensive. The American army would be under French leadership for the next twenty-three days and it would be open warfare, no trenches, no over the top. Once again Sheol (death) will enlarge its throat and open its mouth without measure.

CHAPTER 8

The Second Battle of the Marne

The Second Battle of the Marne lasted from July 15th through August 6th; it was a French-driven, tactical operation while the AEF infantry division generals administered the execution. The AEF classified this as the Aisne-Marne operation: July 18th through August 6th. Within this offensive are The Battle of Soissons, The Battle of the Qurcq, and The Battle of Vesle, (The Second Battle of the Marne is an inverted triangle. Soissons twenty-three miles to the northwest of Chateâu-Thierry and Reims thirty-two miles to the northeast with the base running along the Vesle River from Soissons to Reims, an area of approximately 355 square miles). Within the Aisne-Marne counteroffensive, the 28th Division participated in the front-line two times: The Battle of Qurcq and the Battle of Fismes. It is in the Aisne-Marne operation that for the next twenty-five days the 28th Division will be baptized in combat. It is where Amo, Marcelo, Mauricio, Lute, Moses, Gilbert Harmes, Ruben Vigil, Anastacio Trujillo of the 4th Division, and Joyce Kilmer, of the 42nd Division, would find out if they were promised tomorrow along with three million other men on the Marne.

Germany's Spring Offensive also known as the Kaiser's Battle rolled out about fifty divisions on the Western Front with a series of attacks. The first was on March 21st, through April 5th, near the Somme, codename *Michael*. The second attack was launched at Lys, April 9th through April 27th, where the British and French would lose approximately 200,000 men, codename *Georgette*. The third offensive was at the Aisne, May 27th through June 5th, codename *Gneisenau*. By this time General Pershing was under tremendous pressure by the British and French Generals to incorporate the American troops into their divisions. There was no time for training, the Germans were within fifty miles of Paris, and the British were being threatened to be pushed into the English Channel.

With the German attacks stalled, another German offensive was launched in Champagne-Marne of July 15th through 18th. Again, the German advanced is stopped. The German high command had concluded that it was their last opportunity to deliver the final blow. Unknown to the Allies, this was Germany's last time they would be on the offense. For the next 117 days, they would be on defense, to the end of the war. The Germans would systematically retreat north of the Marne River and reposition themselves in a defensive posture. Fighting alongside and under the French Sixth and Tenth armies were the AEF 1st, 2nd, 3rd, 4th, 26th, 28th, 32nd, and the 42nd U.S. Army divisions, in what would become known as the Second Battle of the Marne.

28th DIVISION (NG)

COMPOSITION

55th Infantry Brigade	**56th Infantry Brigade**	**53d Field Artillery Brigade**
109th Infantry	111th Infantry	107th Field Artillery (75)
110th Infantry (**Amo & Marcelo**)	112th Infantry	108th Field Artillery (155)
108th Machine Gun Battalion	109th Machine Gun Battalion	109th Field Artillery (75
		103d Trench Mortar Battery

Divisional Troops
107th Machine Gun Battalion
103d Engineers
103d Field Signal Battalion
Headquarters Troop

Trains
103d Train Headquarters and Military Police
103d Ammunition Train
103d Supply Train
103d Engineer Train
103d Sanitary Train (Ambulance Companies and
        Field Hospitals 109-112)

ATTACHED

Arty of Fr 39th Div	Aisne-Marne Operation, July 28-31, 1918.
57th FA Brig and 107th Am Tn (32d Div) With 3rd Bn 18th FA Brig (3d Div) attached	Fismes Sector, Aug 7-12, 1918.
107th Engrs (less 1st Bn) and Tn (32d Div)	Fismes Sector, Aug 7-11, 1918.
one aero squadron one bin company	Fismes Sector, Aug 7-17, 1918.
Fr 238th FA (75) Fr 39th Btry 8th Siege Arty (155) one btry Fr 289th Art (280) two btrys 59th CA (6") 12th Aero Sq 1st Bin Co Co B 344th Tank Bn Co E 1st Gas Regt	at times during Meuse-Argonne Operation between Sept 26 and Oct 10, 1918.
327th Inf (82d Div) **Alvin York**	Meuse-Argonne Operation, Sept 29-Oct 3, 1918
164th FA Brig (89th Div)	Thiaucourt Sector, Oct 16-Nov 11, 1918.
134th FA (37th Div)	Thiaucourt Sector, Oct 28-Nov 11, 1918
135th Aero Sq 15th and 69th Bin Cos	Thiaucourt Sector, Nov 10-11, 1918

Source: United States Army Center of Military History. Order of Battle of the United States Land Forces in the
World War: American Expeditionary Forces 2 Vols. Washington D.C. Government Printing Office, 1988

Figure 16. 28th Division National Guard Composition

CHAPTER 9

On the Trail of The Hun

Amo, Marcelo, and other Huerfanos spent the night there on La Canardière Farm on a hill over-looking the Marne, where nights could reach a low of 55 degrees. [44] After settling in, their corporal must have told them, don't get too comfortable, watch out for cooties, for we leave tomorrow. The next day, July 26th, the 110th departed, marched east to St. Eugene, by way of Chateâu-Thierry, a fourteen-mile hike, arriving 6:00 p.m. Author Hervey Allen, a Lieutenant with the 111th Infantry Regiment, 56th Infantry Brigade, 28th Division, wrote about their experiences toward Fismes. He wrote about seeing German dead still floating in the Marne, and horses lying dead with their legs straight up. Herbert Harmes of Gardner who arrived in the Chateâu-Thierry sector around the 25th of June was assigned to bury German and French soldiers. He stated, "this was very disagreeable work with many disgusting details."[45]

The next day at 4 a.m., the 110th departed via marching northwest backtracking from Saint Eugene to Crézancy, Mezy-Moulins, crossing the Marne again to Mont-Saint-Pere. Then they turned northeasterly to Charteves, up the valley past Jaulgonne and Le Charmel finally arriving at Courmont. It was a thirteen-mile march, with their seventy-pound backpacks, in the rain that turned the congested roads into deep gluey mud. In the early hours of the 28th of July, the 110th relieved the French 156th French Infantry of the 39th French Division, in the darkness, with the only illumination from lightning. On their right flank was the 3rd Division, which was just nicknamed "The Rock of the Marne," where they participated in stopping the final German offensive near Chateâu-Thierry. On their left flank was the 42nd Division, where thirty-eight-year-old, Douglas MacArthur had just become a Brigadier General. It takes the 28th Division and the AEF forty-seven days to capture and secure twenty miles from Chateâu-Thierry to Fismes (Fismes a small city between Soissons and Reims), into another valley where the grape is crushed, and no one is promised tomorrow.

CHAPTER 10

Trees, Bois de Grimpettes

"We have always believed, that where the tree falls, there let it lie."

Theodore Roosevelt

The following poem, titled *Trees*, was written by Joyce Kilmer, in 1913, who would become a Sergeant with the 42nd Division (The Rainbow Division). The first major battle for the 28th Division and for Amo, Marcelo, and the other Huerfanos would be in a wooded area called Bois de Grimpettes, Hill 212, just northeast of a village named Courmont; for many Pennsylvanians and Huerfanos it would be their last.

Trees

I think that I shall never see
A poem lovely as a tree.
A tree whose hungry mouth is prest
Against the sweet earth's flowing breast;
A tree that looks at God all day,
And lifts her leafy arms to pray;
A tree that may in summer wear
A nest of robins in her hair;
Upon whose bosom snow has lain;
Who intimately lives with rain.
Poems are made by fools like me,
But only God can make a tree.

Figure 17. Sgt. Joyce Kilmer

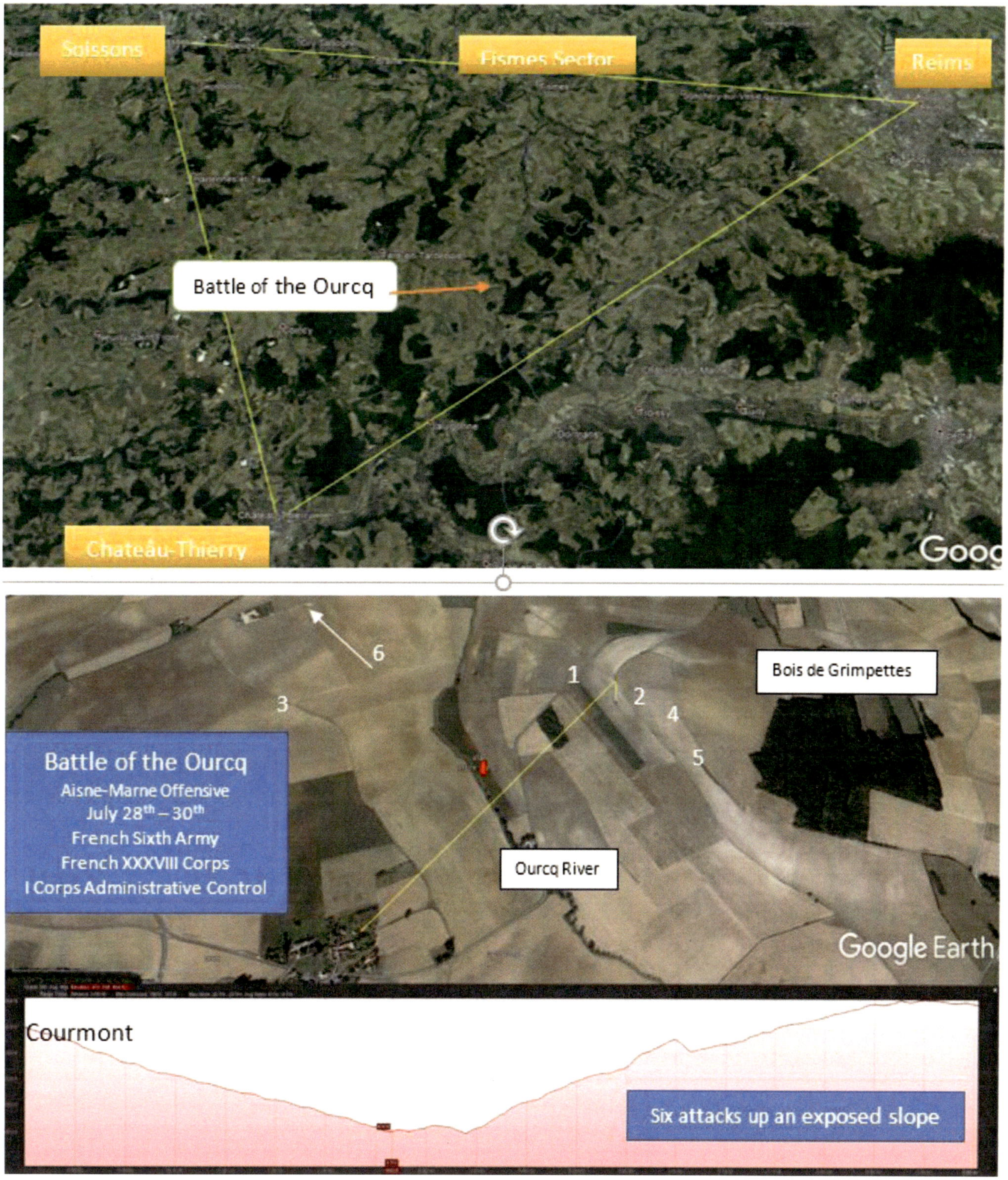

Figure 18. Battle of the Ourcq

1. Pvt. Moses Benavidez, Co. H, Second Battalion., KIA, 29th July, Rouse, CO

2. 2nd Lt. Earl Churchill, Co. F, Second Battalion, KIA, 29th July, Buffalo, NY

3. Pvt. Herbert Harmes, 109th Inf., wounded 29th, July, Gardner, CO

4. Pvt. Mauricio Trujillo, Co. D, First Battalion, wounded, 30th July, Tioga, CO

5. Pvt. Ruben Vigil, Co. G, Second Battalion, wounded, 30th July, Trinidad, CO

6. Sgt. Joyce Kilmer, 165th Inf., 42nd Division, KIA near Seringes-et-Nesles, 30th July, NJ

The next two days and twenty-three hours will forever change the Huerfanos and Pennsylvanians, the majority of whom had never been in the front line or combat. Their mental and physical resolve tested in fire, that is— machine gun fire. The 110th Regiment would experience around fourteen hundred casualties, three hundred killed outright or later died of their wounds. This battle took six attacks before the Germans gave ground, due to poor artillery support. In the last attack on July 30th, with proper artillery support, the 32nd and the 28th Divisions were able to secure Bois des Grimpettes. This battle occurred just twelve miles northeast of Chateâu-Thierry, 1,500 yards northeast of the Ourcq River, between Courmont and Cierges. Most of this land has been returned to farmland and can be seen from the road, D14. One would never know that this was a battlefield and would quickly pass it on the way to some Champagne vineyard.

On Sunday, July 28th, the orders were given to cross the Qurcq River and establish a line 200 yards north of the river. Most rivers in Europe are usually a hundred yards wide, but the fifty-four-mile, northwesterly flowing Qurcq is a tributary of the Marne and was no more than a creek at this time of the year. A reconnaissance officer had crossed it several times before he realized that it was the Qurcq River; it was six feet wide and about a foot deep.

The Battle of Ourcq where the 42nd Division on the left of the 28th Division, had the objective to capture Sergy; the 28th Division in the center to capture Cierges; and the 3rd Division (where Private Mike Duzenack, one of the forty-four braves is with a machine gun battalion) is on the 28th Division right flank, with the objective to capture and secure the Roncheres area. The Germans had the high ground and had created strong defensive positions in a group of woods called Bois de Grimpettes, over a mile wide and three miles in length. Privates Amo, Marcelo, and Lute of Company F; Private Mauricio, Company D; and Private Moses of Company H; of the 110th Regiment, were in line near Courmont. Private Herbert Harmes, Company L was also near this battle with the 109th Regiment, 55th Infantry Brigade.

The Second and Third Battalions were on the line and the First Battalion, Companies A, B, C, and D, in support position. The morning of the 28th the entire regiment was in position and had been taking intermittent shell fire. Shrapnel from one of those shells found a young Pennsylvania Pvt. Harry Moorhead of Company F, killing him that morning.

The Second Battalion occupied the small village of Courmont with the enemy less than 1,500 yards away from their positions. At 3:00 a.m. the Third Battalion engaged at an acute angle (Courmont being the common point) without artillery support and dug in two hundred yards north of and parallel to the Ourcq River. By 4:20 a.m. the crossing was in effect with twelve men killed and sixty-two wounded. Courmont was under severe shell fire at all times and also subjected to a raking machine-gun fire from the hill crests across the river. "Enemy aircraft would dart out of the clouds at frequent intervals, dropping bombs . . ." wrote 1st Lt. Lutz.

This was the 28th Division's first time in battle, and 52-year-old French Brigadier General Jean-Marie Joseph Degoutte of the French Sixth Army wanted to see if the Germans would fight for this area. The 110th Regiment was to attack without artillery support, "with cold steel only."

The Second and Third Battalions charged the hill, an exposed slope. Private Owen M. Serene, 110th Infantry said that "they were immediately met with deadly accurate fire from innumerable machine guns, the bullets seemed 'as thick as flies,' and the troops went down in large numbers."[46] The Second and Third Battalions were forced to retreat to their starting positions. The Germans were not withdrawing and were prepared to hold the line until they could set up their positions at Vesle River, twelve miles northeast of their current stance.

During the attack of July 29th, Amo, Marcelo, and Lute lost their 1st Lt., Earl Churchill of Company F, first thing in the morning. He had just given the orders to advance and started forward when he was hit twice. There he fell, looking at his sergeant, saying, "I'm hit." He died shortly thereafter. Privates Amo, Marcelo, Lute, and Duvigen made it back to attack five more times, but nineteen-year-old Pvt. Moses Benavidez of Company of H did not. When Moses is hit, he is near 2nd Lt. Joseph Ferguson of Company H. Second Lt. Ferguson orders for him to be rescued under heavy fire.[47] By the time they get to Moses, the raking machine-gun fire found him again. Moses was assigned the 25th of July, marched for two days, and in his first attack, it was all over. His parents wouldn't find out until late September that he had been killed in action. He was the son of Felipe Benevidez from Rouse.

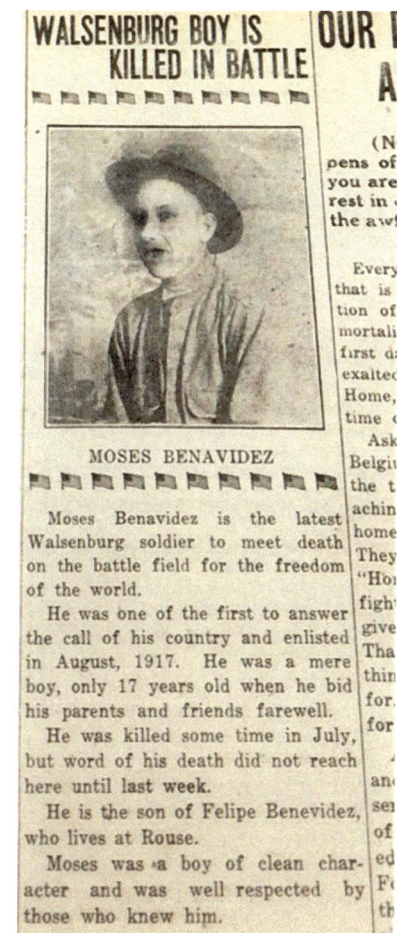

Figure 19. Moses Benavidez

It was not a good day for the Huerfanos; by the end of the day, Pvt. Herbert Harmes and Pvt. Ricardo Archuleta were also wounded. The next day, Tuesday, July 30th, Pvt. Mauricio Trujillo, Co. D of Gardner, and Pvt. Ruben Vigil, Co. G of Trinidad were severely wounded to the extent that they would not return to the war. Also, approximately five miles northwest of Courmont, thirty-one-year-old Sgt. Joyce Kilmer of the 42nd Rainbow Division, a father of five children, was killed by a sniper.

Finally, at 3 p.m., after several attacks with proper artillery support, the 110th Regiment advanced under a rolling barrage and were able to reach their objective. It was now the 32nd Division's turn in the front, and they started relieving the 110th Regiment; relief was completed by nine o'clock Wednesday morning. The 110th Regiment would march three and a half miles back to bivouac in the woods southwest of Le Charmel. There they would rest until August 2nd and march four miles toward Courmont and bivouac for that evening, back on the trail of the Hun. First Lt. Lutz of the 110th Regiment made the following comments regarding the replacements:

> To the replacements who had just recently joined the regiment, the utmost praise must be given. Fully half of these men had been trained for the artillery and knew absolutely nothing about infantry work until called up to take their positions with advancing waves. The advance had to be made up slopes of a hill 700 meters to the crest and over ground affording no protection whatsoever. [48]

General Degoutte was not looked upon favorably for not providing adequate artillery support, the officers of the 28th Division felt that life was sacrificed needlessly; nevertheless, the 110th Regiment incorporated into their records General Degoutte's commendation:

> . . . The young divisions which entered the battle for the first time showed their possession of a dignity in keeping with the war traditions of the Regular Army. They have the same ardent will to defeat the Boche and the same discipline which guarantees that an order given by the Chief will always be executed whatever the difficulties be encountered and whatever sacrifices have to be made . . . [49]

Herbert Harmes, who joined the army from Gardner, and who was badly wounded in France some weeks ago, returned home the first of the week on a furlough.

Mr. Harmes was shot thru his right arm and also througu his leg, but the splendid care he received has brought him safely thru and his many friends are more than glad to have him back home for a short stay.

He has but twenty days here, and then must report to San Francisco.

Figure 20. Herbert Harmes

CHAPTER 11

Rendezvous with Death

". . . I have a rendezvous with death on some scarred slope of battered hill . . . I shall not fail that rendezvous."

— Alan Seeger, February 1916, French Foreign Legion, KIA July 4, 1916, France

From their relief of the front line, August 1st through August 11th, and marching back toward the front line over twenty-nine enlisted men were killed, and 103 wounded by constant shelling. After they had bivouacked in the woods near Le Charmel on August 1st, a German plane dropped six monster bombs in the camp, killing twenty-two and wounding eighty. The 110th Regiment continued its drive northeasterly behind the 32nd Division, known as "Iron Jaws," marching through Courmont again. It was there where they had their first big battle as a division. They were now on their way to an area called the Fismes Sector, small villages between Soissons and Reims on the Vesle River. On their march back to the front line, they spent one day in Courmont where they had just fought days before. "A veritable slaughter house, unburied dead, both American and German, as well as horses, and mules . . ."[50] wrote 1st Lt. Lutz. If it wasn't the German shelling, it was the stench, flies, blistering heat one moment, sheets of rain the next, till they were soaked. They marched through Cierges and Chamery where Quentin Roosevelt had been killed twenty-one days earlier. The Germans had buried him and set up a marker for Quentin out of respect for former President Theodore Roosevelt.

From Chamery they marched north through Coulonges-Cohan, to Cohan where they spent one night where it started to rain, along with constant German shelling. The next day they moved north of Dravegny in a ravine, just three miles south of Saint Gilles. Here between the 6th and the 11th of August, the book cover photograph was probably taken of Amo and Marcelo, having perhaps their first taste of champagne or sour red wine. They most likely had to share the bottle with the rest of the platoon. That any fermented spirits survived the German occupation, and then the 32nd Division, was highly unlikely. Most troops complained about finding empty dusty bottles with spiders, especially in this sector of France. This photograph finds them together again, adventurous, clean, and rested with the vigor of youth; Amo is twenty-three and Marcelo twenty-two, the last known photo of Amo. Amo writes a letter from this area and it is printed in *The Independent,* October 18, 1918.

Somewhere in France
August 9, 1918

Dear Folks:

Just dropping you this few lines to let you know that I am o.k., and hope you are all well.
Cousin M. O. R. is here and we are very happy.

With best wishes.
John.

Figure 21. Amo and Marcelo wine tasting

First cousins Amo and Marcelo officially combat soldiers; enjoying a bouteille of French wine. Photo most likely taken near Saint-Gilles, Marne Department, ca. August 6th- 11th, 1918.

Figure 22. Marcelo fourth from the left

Courtesy of Reynolds grandchildren

Figure 23. 110th near St. Gilles France

Photo from the 110th Association

Figure 24. Marcelo sets his sights while near Dravegny

Courtesy of Reynolds grandchildren

The two pictures with Marcelo seem to reflect this area and time between Dravegny and Saint Gilles.[51] The probability of having a picture taken was so unlikely; these photos may have been taken by the Signal Corps. Cameras were banned for most of AEF, *The Stars and Stripes*, February 15, 1918: reports "No photographs will be taken in the zone of the American armies except by the official photographers . . ." and reiterated in the August 2nd, 1918, *Star and Stripes* "Ban on Cameras Strict as Ever." The ban wasn't lifted until the following year.

On August the 12th, the 110th Regiment started for the front line, east of Fismes, near Courville, south of the Vesle River. Privates Amo, Marcelo, Lute, and Dewgen would be in this area for the next twenty-seven days, becoming part of the newly formed First Army, August 10th. The AEF designated this period as the Oise-Aisne Offensive from August 18th through September 9th. Going into relief was the 42nd Division replaced by the 77th Division and the 32nd Division and French 152nd Regiment substituted by the 28th Division. The Germans held on tightly to this area and had strong defensive positions; they would hold this area until October 11th.

CHAPTER 12

The Runner

"... snatch 'em up ... Tis sport to maul a runner,"

— Scarus, Antony and Cleopatra [IV,7].

Private Amo Vigil became a designated runner probably after the Battle of Bois des Grimpettes when many positions needed to be filled. The records show that he was a Brigade Runner versus a battalion or company runner; if so, that means he would deliver messages / orders to battalion runners who would then give them to company runners. Pvt. George Herring from Iowa was a runner also with 90th Division and George Herring Jr. wrote it was "perhaps the most dangerous job the Army because it required leaving the relative safety of the trenches of dugouts and being exposed to enemy artillery, machine guns, and strafing from aircraft." [52] Amo entered an age-old, world tradition of running messages like the legendary 5th century BC Athenian messenger Pheidippides, a 1st millennium BC Benjamite from Israel who ran from the battle line, clothes torn and dust on his head to report that the Ark was captured.[53] A runner contemporary with Amo was twenty-nine-year-old Adolf Hitler for the Germans. Historians had not distinguished between regimental runners, a relatively safe job versus being a battalion or a company runner who had to be calm and courageous under machine-gun and artillery fire. A runner was usually young and slim and could run like the wind, fleet-winged duty; that ride upon the violent speed of fire, swifter than eagles. The *Stars and Stripes*, ran this article August 9, 1918, page one:

Figure 25. John "Amo" Vigil, ca. 1917-18, picture may have been taken at Camp Kearney

Courtesy of Reynolds grandchildren

Speedy Runners North of Ourcq Race with Death

The runners are the fleet youngsters who, as the battle sways and strains, keep regiment in touch with the battalion, battalion with company, company with platoon. To let each unit know how the others are faring, above all in such fighting as the last weeks have seen, to let the nervous guns know to what line the surging Infantrymen have attained, this is the business of the runners. That device is the human messenger, the runner of the battlefield. Most of them are young men of eighteen or nineteen. Their work is important beyond measure. It is dangerous because sometimes they cannot crouch and take cover . . . Sometimes the path was so perilous and word so vital that three were charged with one message.

On the left flank of the 110th Regiment was the 56th Infantry Brigade, 111th Regiment, which was already fighting in the village of Fismes. The 110th Regiment entered the line between two villages Fismes and Magneux, two miles east of Fismes along the Vesle River. The front line was approximately 200 yards south of the Vesle River, and in this area the brave Huerfano privates along with the Pennsylvanians continue to apply pressure to the Germans. From the 12th through 26th of August, the 110th Battalions and the Germans jabbed at each other over a sector which both armies did not consider that strategic. But the Germans held the line, and the 110th Battalions continued to probe in order to establish another bridgehead. On the 26th of August, the Second Battalion relieved the Third Battalion, near the village of Magneux. On this day Private Dewgen Leyba, of Gardner, was wounded along with thirty-three other men.[54] The next two days were relatively quiet compared to the 26th; the length of daylight was over fifteen hours and the days were hot, with plenty of flies and bees. The food was tainted salmon, and water was scarce.

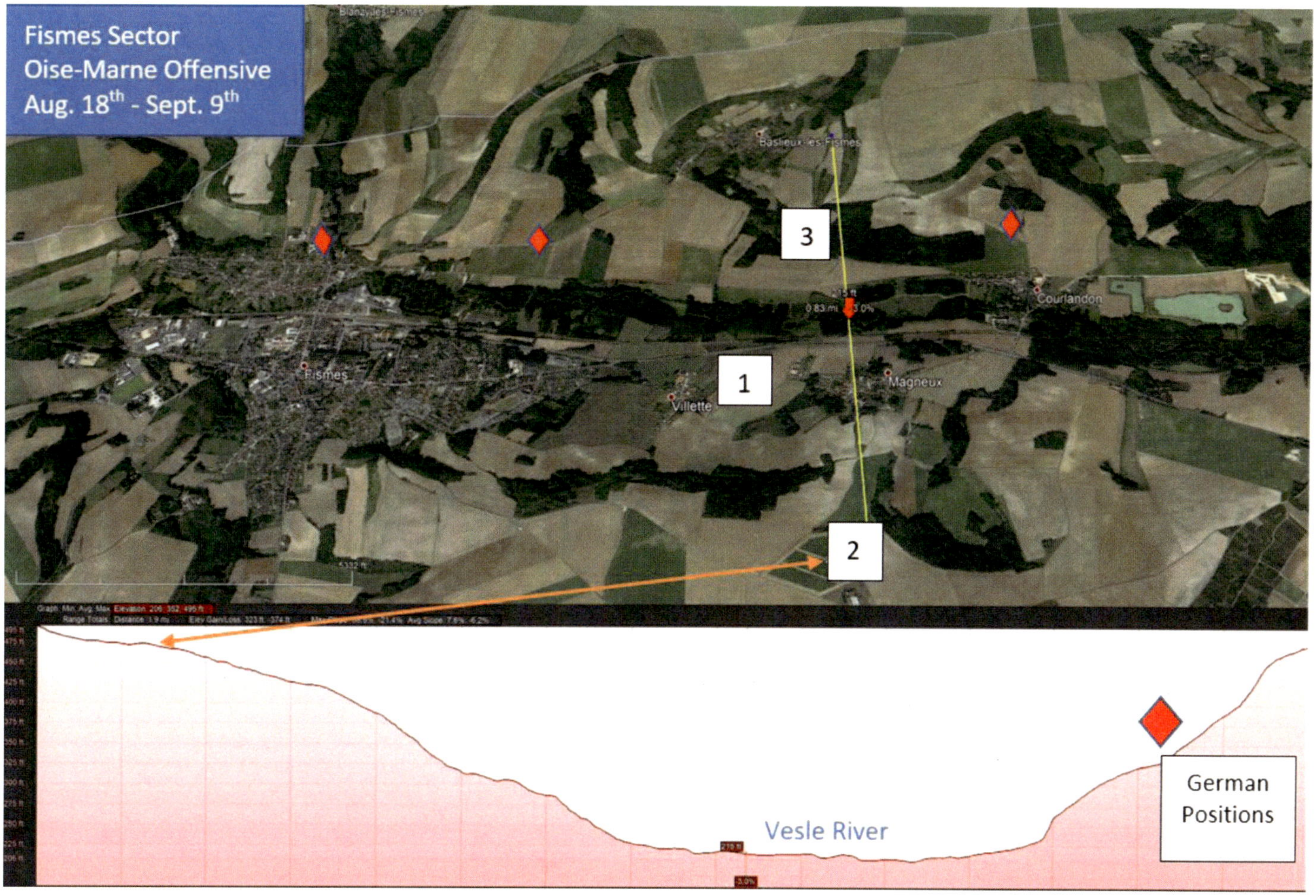

Fismes Sector
Oise-Marne Offensive
Aug. 18th - Sept. 9th

German Positions

Vesle River

Figure 26. Fismes Sector, hallow ground

1. Pvt. Dewgen Leyba, Co. M, Second Battalion, wounded 26th of August

2. Pvt. Amo Vigil, Co. F, Second Battalion, KIA Friday, 30th of August

3. Pvt. Lute Cordova, Co. F, Second Battalion, wounded 6th of September

Coincidentally on Friday, August 30th, Marcelo made the front page of *The Independent*, a reminder to the family that their sons were in France. Mrs. Joseph Reynolds, Manuelita, had just received a card from Marcelo that his ship had arrived safely. It took about fifty days for Manuelita to get that card; he had landed in Liverpool on July 9th. As the Huerfano County Vigils and Reynolds were starting their day, it is eight hours ahead in France, by lunchtime in Huerfano County Amo had "gone west," a euphemism for a soldier who had been killed.

MARCELLO OTTO REYNOLDS
13th Co., Overseas Casuals

Mrs. Jaseph Reynolds received a card from her son, Marcello, from Somewhere in France, saying, "The ship upon which I sailed has arrived safely overseas." He left Walsenburg October 3, 1917.

Figure 27. Marcelo Reynolds, front page, August 30, 1918

It was just another hot day on the front line, intermittent artillery duels, waiting for the next advance, when an incoming shell found Amo, killing him instantly. Here is a portion of the poem, "The Woods called it Rouge-Bouquet," written by Sgt. Joyce Kilmer, in France of March 1918. He dedicated it to the memory of nineteen soldiers who made the supreme sacrifice at Rouge-Bouquet, Forest of Parroy, France, March 7th. *The Stars and Stripes* posted it August 16, 1918, page six, shortly after he been killed on July 30th.

. . . There is new-made grave today,

Built by never a spade nor pick,

Yet covered with earth ten meters thick.

There lie many fighting men,

Dead in their youthful prime,

Never to laugh nor to live again

Nor taste the summer time;

For death came flying through the air

And stopped his flight at the dugout stair,

Touched his prey—

and left them there—

Clay to clay.

He hid their bodies stealthy

In the soil of the land they sought to free,

And fled away . . ..

An eyewitness Pvt. Joseph E. Strittmatter, of Company F, gave the following statement:

Pvt. John A. Vigil, while on post as Brigade Runner, was hit by a shell and instantly killed on August 30, 1918. This was about 1,000 yards south of Magneux. He was buried close to where he was killed.[55]

The story was told had Marcelo not gone for water, he would have been killed also.

GRAVE OF 28TH DIVISION SOLDIER KILLED JULY 29, 1918
This burial was made by buddies. Note use of helmet, rifle and pack.

Photo from the 110th Association

Amo's parents Damacio and Margarita were notified sometime in late October that Amo was wounded and notice was posted in the newspaper October 24th. On the 17th of October Herbert Harmes spoke at the Star Theater where many Huerfanos came to hear him talk about his war experience. Herbert mentions Amo and Marcelo were last seen July 29th, which would have been near Courmont. By the time Amo's parents get the notice, the Meuse-Argonne battle was already into twenty-nine days out of forty-five. Damacio and Margarita wouldn't find out that Amo was killed until December 20th.

There were still two Huerfanos left, Marcelo and Lute both with Company F, and the war had no end in sight.

The 110th Regiment remained in the front line for the next eight days and advanced another two miles north crossing the Vesle by Villette when relieved on the September 8th. Upon that advance, Lute Cordova is wounded on September 6th.[56] Lute would not rejoin the company until December 1918. Out of the group of the Huerfano forty-four brave, Marcelo would be one of the few to see the whole war through without being wounded or killed. The Oise-Aisne Campaign was over for the 28th Division; for the next eighteen days they would be moving and reorganizing for the next offensive. In just forty-six days he was already involved in two military campaigns, the Aisne-Marne Offensive, and the Oise-Aisne Operation. It would be the last time most U.S. Army divisions would fight under French tactical direction.

CHAPTER 13

Moving and Marching

Now the 110th Regiment moved from the Fismes sector to Arcis-le-Ponsart five miles south, arriving at 11:30 a.m. where they boarded trucks and were taken to the vicinity of Abbey d'lgny where they deloused, bathed, and put on new uniforms. There they bivouacked east of Maison Forestière until the ninth. On the tenth, they were on the move again toward Oeuilly, a thirteen-mile southeasterly march, once more in the rain. At 6 p.m. they marched to Boursault and embussed at 9 p.m. for a sixty-mile eastbound ride through Epernay, Chalons-en-Champagne; the Second Battalion arrived in Mussey the next day and bivouacked. The 28th Division did not participate in the Battle of Saint-Mihiel, 12th through 16th of September, the Verdun Front, which was a major U.S. Army success. The Saint-Mihiel offensive caught the Germans by surprise as they were moving to reinforce the Meuse-Argonne sector due to a buildup of American forces in that area.

Delousing plant at Abby d'Igny, France.

On the 17th of September, the 110th Regiment started moving north toward Forest DeLavers, bivouacked, and then on the 19th they bivouacked north of Les Islettes where four days earlier Marcelo had turned twenty-three and on the 19th of September had his first wedding anniversary. The next morning, 4 o'clock they started moving again, a two-mile march northeast and then bivouacked just to the southeast of Locheres for the next five days. There was no doubt that by the movement and congestion of troops that they were ramping up for another major campaign. It would be the Meuse-Argonne Offensive, a joint American-French operation.

By this time the whole First Army was getting into position, the I Corps composed from right to left: the 35th, the 28th, and the 77th Divisions. Future U.S. President, thirty-four-year-old Captain Harry Truman was with Battery D, 129th Field Artillery, 35th Division, also known as the Santa Fe Division. Destined to be a WWII General, but now a Lt. Colonel, George S. Patton Jr. had a brigade of 140 tanks, and they would fight alongside the 28th and 35th Divisions.

The First American Army's twenty-five-mile front was between the Argonne Forest and Verdun.[57] Marcelo and the Second Battalion of the 110th Regiment would follow the Aire River north to Chatel-Chéhéry where they would be relieved by 82nd Division on October 9th. The 82nd Division became famous because of the actions taken by Corporal Alvin York, on October 8[th,] for which was awarded a Congressional Medal of Honor. By the 26th of September, the First Army was in position. From right to left was the French Fourth Army, the U.S. First Army with three Corps: I Corps, V Corps, III Corps, and to the far left the French XVII Corps; objective, the railroad center of Sedan, forty miles due north.

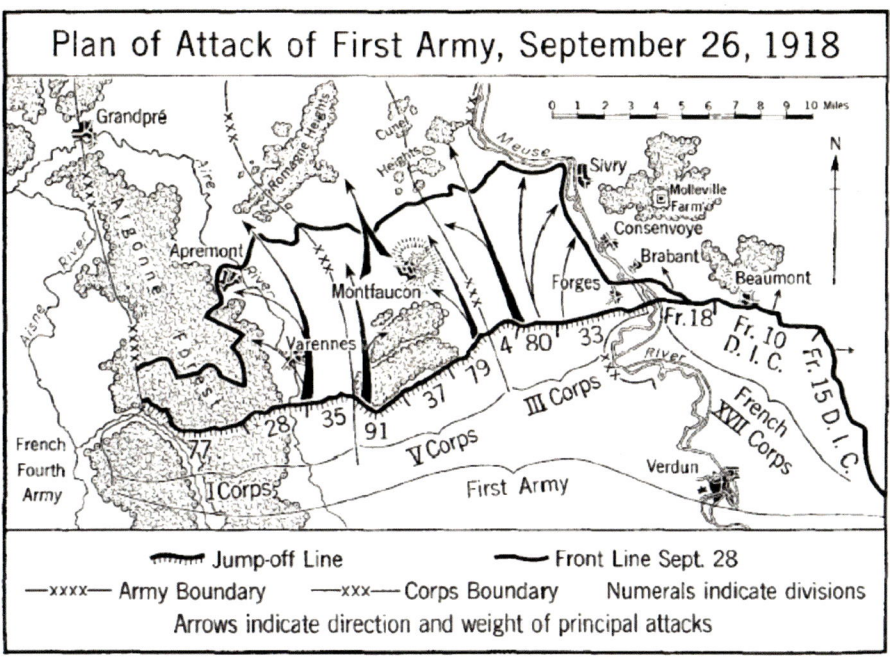

Figure 28. Plan of Attack, September 26, 1918

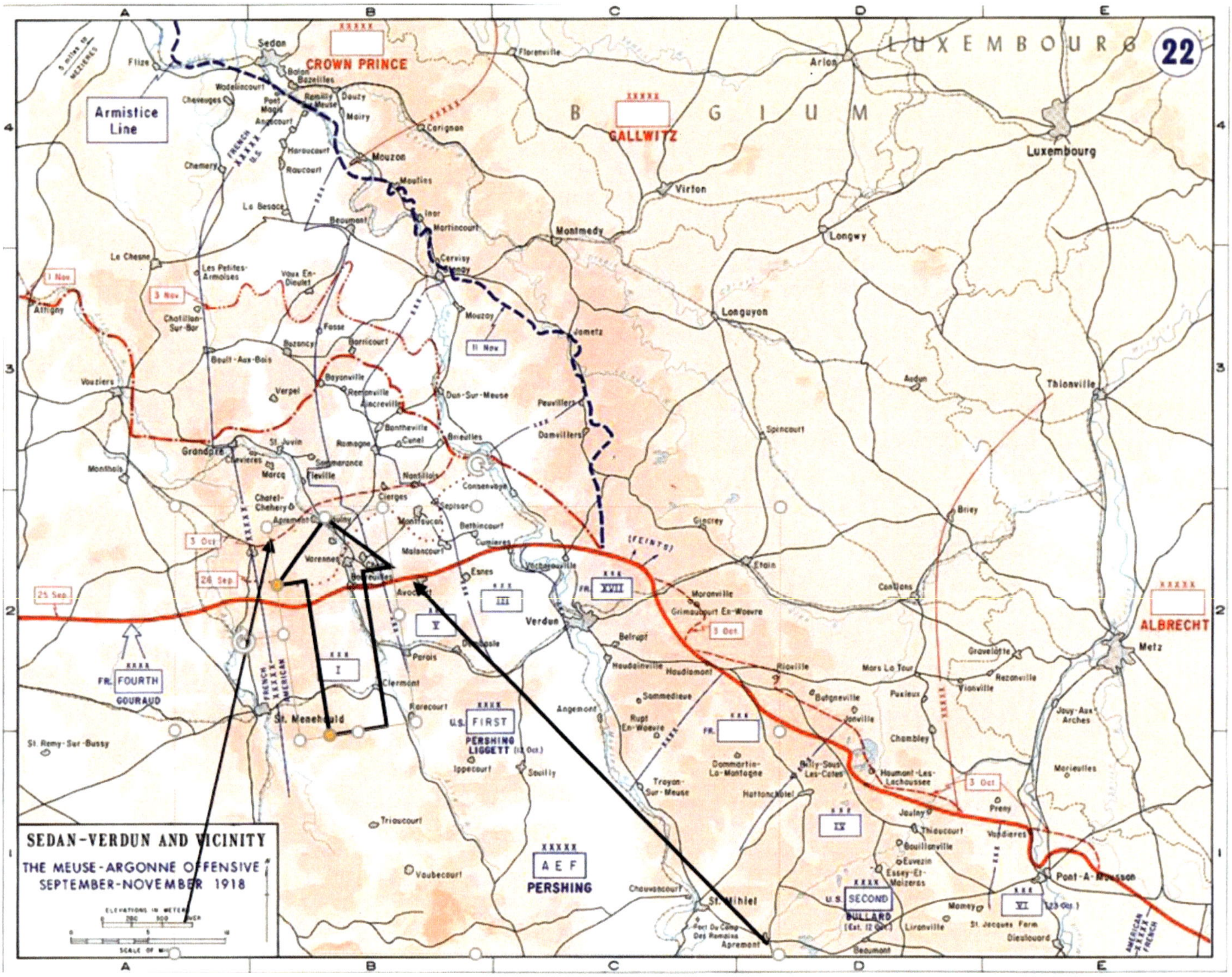

Figure 29. Meuse-Argonne Offensive

https://westpoint.edu/sites/default/files/inlineimages/academics/
academic_departments/history/WWI/WWOn

Maj. C. Whittlesey   *Corp. A. York*   *Pvt. M. Reynolds*   *Capt. H Truman*   *Lt. Col. G. Patton Jr.*

Fourteen Days in October

On Thursday, September 26, 1:30 a.m., the artillery commenced, a barrage from one end of the earth to the other, lighting up the sky. A heavy mist laid over H-hour, set for five-thirty in the morning. Marcelo, the 110th Regiment, and nine American divisions, 225,000 men emerged from their positions. Marcelo and the Second Battalion would follow the First Battalion, with the Third Battalion in reserve. They were less than a mile south of Neuvilly-en Argonne to the left bank of the Aire River from their start off point.

Awaiting Marcelo and the 110th Regiment was barbed wire, tank traps, and mined roads. On their left was the Argonne Forest where the Germans held the high ground, first position: rusty barbed wire hidden in nature's undergrowth, sacrificial machine-gun units, and it seemed the intermediate area had a cannon for every square foot. If a German didn't have a machine gun, they had a cannon.

Marcelo advanced 3.3 miles through Neuvilly-en-Argonne and arrived at Boureuilles by 10 a.m. With the mist lifting, the German fire became more intense and more accurate. When Lt. Colonel George S. Patton Jr. went toward the front to find out why the tanks weren't advancing, he was little more than a mile east of Marcelo's position. Lt. Colonel Patton was encouraging his troops to keep pressing forward near Cheppy, when shrapnel found him, hitting him around his midriff and cutting short his path to glory the first day, just five hours into the battle. He was temporarily knocked out but regained consciousness long enough to reorganize his sector before being taken to the hospital. Tanks fighting with the 28th Division ran into concrete pillboxes for the first time and silenced them by firing straight into the gun slits. Tankers with 35th Division helped capture a strongpoint at Vauquois and also one at Cheppy. The 304th Brigade lost 43 tanks that day.[58] By 11:30 a.m. the 110th Regiment arrived in Varennes and by 2:30 p.m. advanced another mile north of Varennes, the I Corps objective for the 28th Division. Marcelo's Second Battalion was in support of the First Battalion, and they had penetrated over six miles their first day. Today the war was over for Lt. Colonel Patton and for sixteen enlisted men killed, forty-one wounded, and four missing from the 110th Regiment.

The next day, Friday, September 27th, a treacherous day, the regiment attacked at 6 a.m. First Battalion continued to be in front, supported by the Second Battalion, and they arrived in Montblainville at 10:30 a.m., advancing a mile and a half. Marcelo and Company F were assigned 200 yards west of Varennes-Montblainville road, where they encountered heavy crossfire. Company F lost two sergeants and a corporal to machine gun fire in the area. Due to the 110th Regiment flanks being exposed, the Germans counter-attacked at 11:30 a.m., but were thrown back with heavy losses. The Germans attacked again at 3 p.m. and Company G of the Second Battalion used captured German machine guns to repel the German onslaught and was able to hold their positions, where both counter-attacks left many dead. First Lt. Lutz wrote "the dead were piled two deep in a small orchard . . . ."[59] No hand-to-hand combat was mentioned, but it was close. By the end of the day, the 110th Regiment was 300 yards north of Montblainville with thirty-eight enlisted men killed, one-hundred-seventy-nine wounded, and ten missing.

The 28th of September through 1st of October should be known as the Battle of Apremont. September 28th finds Marcelo ready to go by 6 a.m. Second and Third Battalions take the lead in capturing Apremont, two miles north of Montblainville. They are repulsed the first time, due to a narrow passage between the river and a cliff surmounted by numerous machine guns. The second assault succeeded by coordination of the artillery and tanks; the battalions did a direct assault over a plateau. By 4 p.m. they took the town and established a line 300 yards north of Apremont.

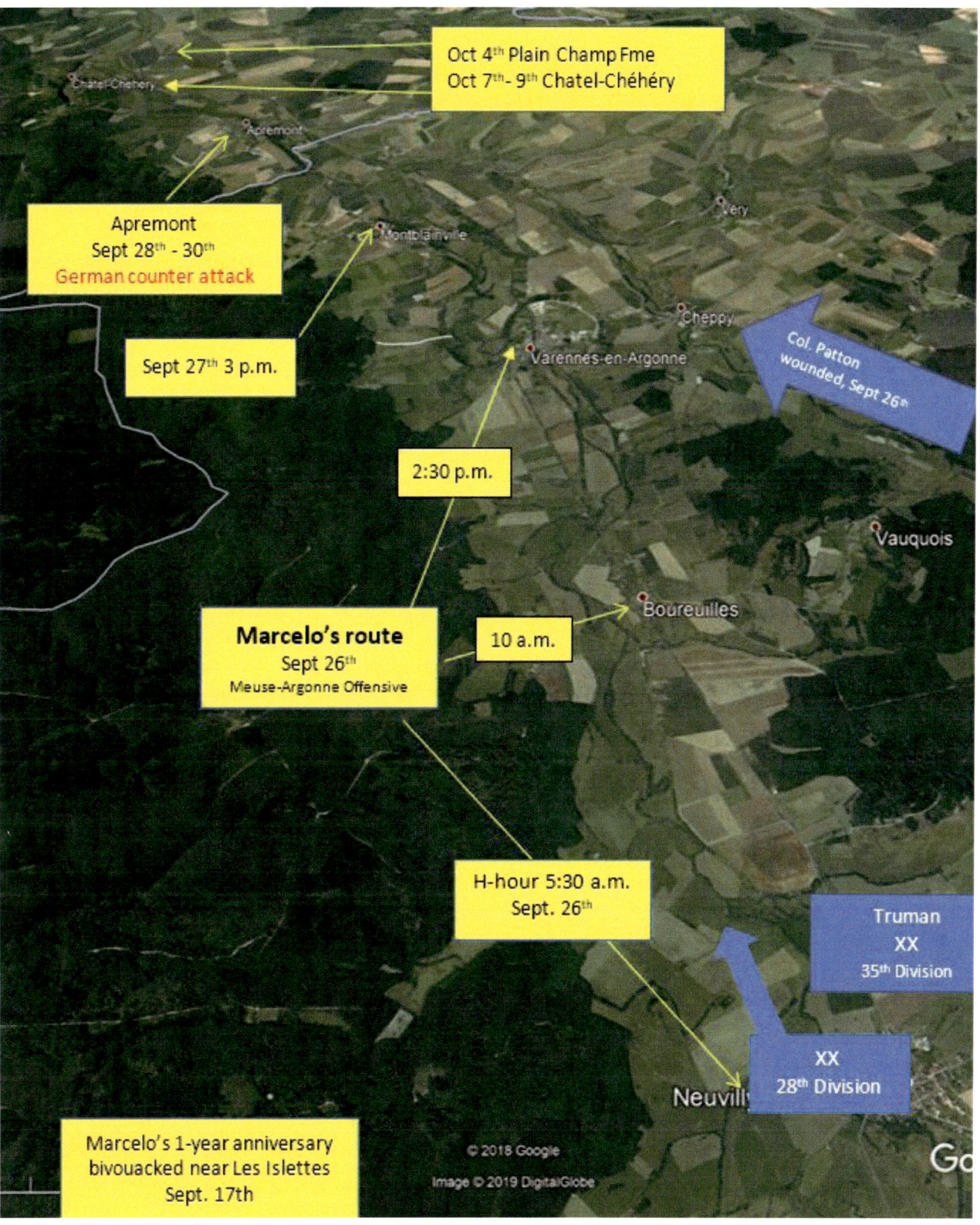

Figure 30. Marcelo Reynolds in the Meuse-Argonne Offensive

At the end of the day, fourteen enlisted men were dead, one-hundred and forty to two-hundred-sixty-five wounded, and nine missing. One officer killed on the September 28th, was 2nd Lt. Joseph Ferguson, of Company H, Second Battalion, from Philadelphia, Pennsylvania who had tried to rescue Moses Benavidez when Benavidez was wounded.

The 110th Regiment had secured Apremont, and the Third Battalion was ordered to relieve the front line at 7 p.m., but during the relief a German Regiment counterattacked. "The attack was preceded by a heavy machine gun and artillery barrage and pushed with great resolution," said captured 110th Regiment battalion officers. Surprise and fury were the words used by the First and Second Battalion soldiers; the Germans wanted this town back due to its strategic importance. Marcelo late in his life spoke of being caught and separated from his company behind a German counter-attack when a mortally wounded German soldier walked toward him and fell on Marcelo before dying. Marcelo lay down and covered himself with the German soldier until the German onslaught receded. It is in this battle and village that this incident most likely occurred.

Tuesday, October 1st, the 110th Regiment remained at the front line with the Third Battalion to lead in the new attack at 6 a.m., Second Battalion in support, and the First Battalion in reserve. But the Germans seemed to know of the advance and commenced with a barrage and attacked at 5:45 a.m. in large numbers. By 8:00 a.m. the counter attack was over, men and machines were worn out, and the 110th held the village. The 109th Infantry relieved the 110th and Marcelo went south of Apremont to regroup. During these eighty-nine hours in and around Apremont, fifty-four men were killed in action, fifty-one of them enlisted men. A total of 342 men were wounded, and another fifty-three were missing in action. The next few days south of Apremont within proximity to the front line, five enlisted men were killed, sixty-six wounded, and five missing. While the 110th Regiment was regrouping three miles to their left, the 77th Division was attacking in the Argonne Forest. Unknown to the 77th Division, 308th Battalion, their flanks had been exposed due to a massive German counter attack stalling the French on their right. Their left flank was also experiencing resistance and was not in position, leaving Major Whittlesey and 550 men to be encircled by the Germans. Whittlesey and his men become known as the "Lost Battalion." By October 7th they were rescued, and the 550 American troops had been reduced to 194, due to being captured, killed, or missing in action. Although Major Whittlesey was recognized for his outstanding leadership, a Medal of Honor recipient, he never recovered from the war. Days after the third anniversary of that battle, he put his personal affairs in order before going on a cruise to Havana. After dinner and drinks with some other passengers, he quietly walked into the darkness of the night and jumped overboard.

October 3rd finds two enlisted men killed, twenty-three wounded, and three missing while in reserve. On October 4th, the Second Battalion will advance north of Apremont with the Aire River on their left and Fleville-Baulny on their right, one and one-half miles to Plain Champ Fme. There was heavy fighting all day: nine enlisted men killed, forty-eight wounded, and eight missing. October 5th saw more of the same, continuous battle all day in the same area, with two enlisted men killed, thirty-five wounded, and seven missing. October 6th, friendly and enemy artillery were very active, six enlisted men killed, thirty wounded, and two missing. During this time the 82nd Division was used from September 29th to October 3rd to support the 28th Division and helped stiffen the lines of the 35th Division near Baulny.

Monday, October 7th, Marcelo, the 110th and the 112th Regiments, and elements of the 82nd Division attacked at 5:30 a.m., crossed the Aire River between La Forge during the night and occupied Chatel-Chéhéry.

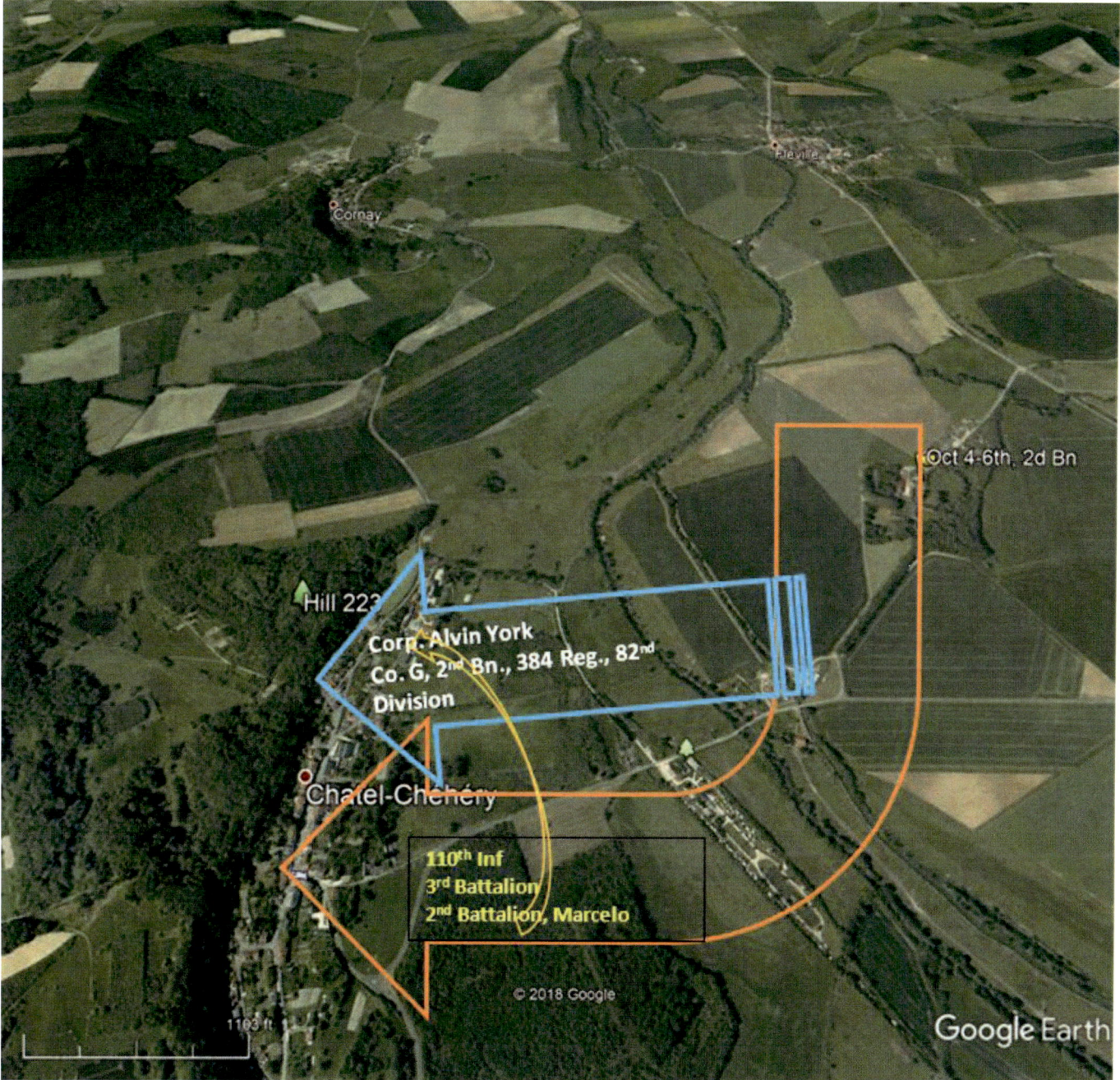

Figure 31. Marcelo Reynolds and Alvin York at Chatel-Chéhéry

Marcelo and the Second Battalion and thirty-one-year-old Corporal Alvin York, Company G, 328th Infantry Regiment, 82nd Division, from Tennessee, the conscientious objector were within yards of each other. The following is 1st Lt. Lutz's account on the battle:

> The 82nd Division was unable...to get one regiment up in time and left a gap in the line. On the north of the town Hill 223 had not been taken by the 82nd Division... and the right of the 110th was suffering severely from machine gun fire...therefore the Second Battalion advanced on the hill. The Machine Gun Company and one-pounders opened a heavy fire on the crest of the hill, keeping the Germans there under cover while the infantry men climbed a steep cliff hand over hand. As they reached the top the covering fire ceased and our men met the Germans with a bayonet.[60]

The action taken by the Second Battalion contributed to Alvin York's success that day, but nothing is mentioned of the Second Battalion of the 110th moving into that gap other than 1st Lt. Lutz account stated above. In the *History of Three Hundred and Twenty-Eight Regiment of Infantry of the Eighty Second Division, A.E.F.* on page forty-five, they record that there is a gap between the 327th and the 328th on that same day:

> . . . the 110th Infantry on the left, all driving west for the corps objective . . . The advance continued with slight resistance for about 700 meters, but then met with withering machine gun fire from the front and both flanks. It developed that the original assignment of sectors left a gap of a kilometer between the 327th and 328th, so that our attack was launched with both flanks exposed. The advance continued, however, in spite of these most adverse conditions until 11:30, when it was utterly impossible to proceed further without flank protection.[61]

Alvin York who was is in the same vicinity remarked in his account, October 7th:

> We lay in some little holes by the roadside all day. That night we went and stayed a little while and come back to our little holes and the shells busting [sic] all around us. I saw men just blown up by the big German shells. So the order came for us to take hills 223 and 240 the 8th. It was raining a little bit all day, drizzly and very damp. Lots of big shells bursting all around us.[62]

That morning Marcelo and Second Battalion attacked hill 223, covering Corporal York's right flank where they turned west. As Marcelo and the Second Battalion attacked hill 223, by 6:10 a.m. Corporal York was into the beginning of a two-mile trek coming and going.

So on the morning of the 8th, just before daylight, we started for the hill of Chatel-Chehery [sic]. So before we got there it got light, and the Germans sent over a heavy barrage and also gas, and we put on our gas masks and just pressed right on thought those shells and got to the top of Hill 223 to where we were to start over the top at 6:10 AM. And they was to give us a barrage. So the time came, and no barrage, and we had to start without one. So as we started over the top at 6:10 A.M., and the Germans was putting their machines guns to work all over the hill in front of us and on our left and right. So I was in support and I could see my pals getting picked off until it almost looked like there was none left. Corporal Alvin York[63]

Corporal York would go on to capture 132 German soldiers, and by the end of the day he would be Sergeant Alvin York. Marcelo may have been an eyewitness to Corporal York bringing in captured German troops that morning. Corporal York became a Medal of Honor recipient due to his actions, where countless lives of Germans and Americans were spared in the Chatel-Chéhéry hills that one day.

Figure 32. 28th Division being rotated out from the front-line
National Archives

The next day the situation was unchanged except for the casualty list, fifteen enlisted men killed, sixty-seven wounded, and twenty-three missing. That was it for Marcelo and the 28th Division. They would be relieved by the 82nd Division on October 9th and relief was completed by 5:30 a.m. Their fight after fourteen days in the Meuse-Argonne was over; however, six enlisted men were killed, four wounded, and twelve missing. This photo shows men from the 28th Division being rotated out, probably coming from Chatel-Chéhéry: As fresh troops passed them going to the front, they would yell out "Better make your peace with your Jesus, fellows, before you go up there."[64]

CHAPTER 15

The Thiaucourt Sector

Marcelo and the 110th marched eight miles back through Apremont, Montblainville, Varennes-en-Argonne, Boureuilles, and bivouacked near Camp de Buzon. The next day they marched to Neuvilly-en-Argonne, another two miles south where they embussed around 4:30 p.m., Marcelo and the Second Battalion's destination was Fme. de St. Charles, near Royaumiex, a forty-seven-mile southeast bus ride arriving October 11th, where they would report to the IV Corps, Second Army.

On October 12th, Marcelo's unit moved to the Royaumiex area and bivouacked there until October 17th when at noon they marched to Rambucourt, a seven-mile northwesterly march. Also, that same day in Huerfano County, Herbert Harmes gave a speech at the Star Theatre in Walsenburg talking about his experiences. The Second Battalion bivouacked at Rambucourt until October 28th. It was at this time the Vigils got notice that Amo was wounded; they probably assumed that he was wounded in Meuse-Argonne, but there were no details.

Marcelo and the Second Battalion would be embussed at 3:30 p.m. and proceeded to Heudicourt arriving at 5 p.m., an eleven-mile trip. Marcelo would then march over six miles to the front line where on the 29th they would relieve the 146th French Infantry northeast of Bois de Chaufour. The next couple of days October 30th through November the 3rd, the sector was reported as very quiet, but patrols were active. Monday, November 4th through the 11th, Marcelo and the Second Battalion would be on patrol verifying if the Germans were still in the area. However, most of the AEF, wherever they were on the front line, were still attacking even though both sides knew that a truce was pending. At 3:30 a.m., November 11th, the Second Battalion was in support of the 109th in Bois de la Grande Souche to attack the enemy line northeast of Haumont at dawn.

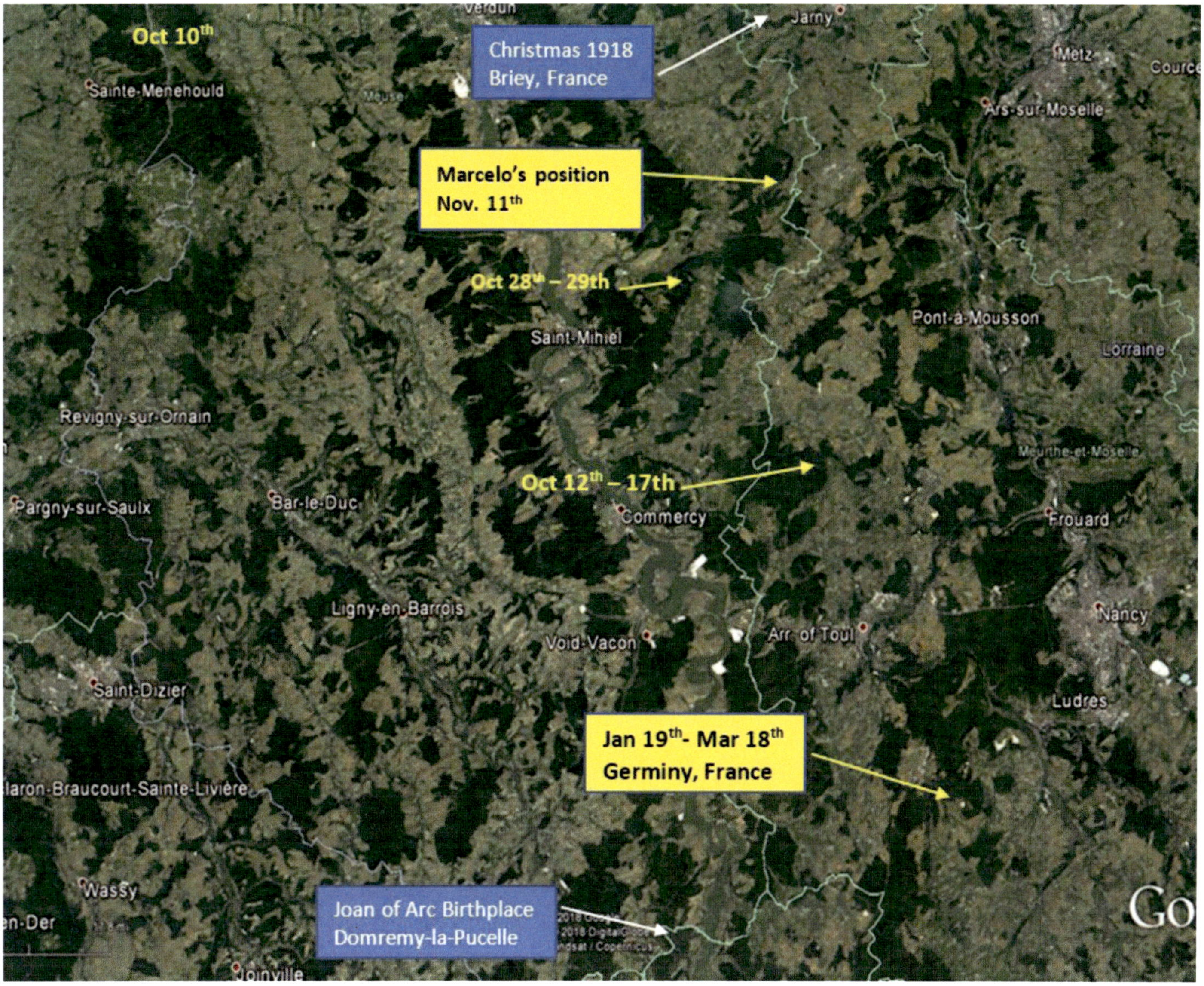

Figure 33. Marcelo Reynolds position on November 11th War is Over

Oct 10th The Meuse Campaign is over for the 28th Division, embussed 47 miles south to Fme de. St. Charles.

Oct 12th Second Battalion in Royaumiex; Oct 17th to Rambucourt, seven-mile march; Oct 28th to Heudicout.

Nov 11th Second Battalion and Marcelo north of Saint-Benoît en Woëvre when Armistice is signed.

Dec 25th Christmas 1918 in Briey, seven miles north of Jarny.

Jan 19th – Mar 18th, Stationed in Germiny France, where Company F takes a photo.

Joan of Arc birthplace, ca. 1412, a travel destination for soldiers stationed in the area.

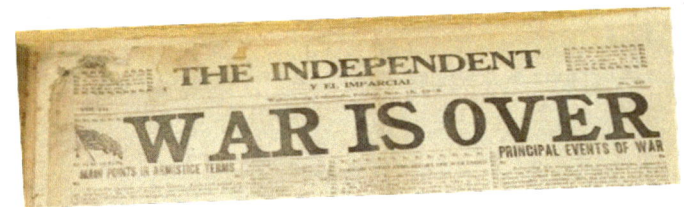

Figure 34. War is Over

Word was received at 8:48 a.m. that Armistice had been signed and that hostilities would cease after 11:00 a.m., so the advance troops stopped and dug in where they were till November 20th, when they withdrew. On the 22nd of November, Marcelo and Second Battalion left the Bois le Chaufour. The next stop was Maison-Forestière when the question must have occurred, when do we go home? Until the answer came, there was policing, inspections, and maneuvers where they occupied the same positions until December 9th.

On the 9th of December, Marcelo and the Second Battalion left Bois de Creue and marched twelve miles northeasterly via St. Benoit and Chambley to Mars-la-Tour, arriving there at 3 p.m. They departed the next day and marched eleven miles through Jarny and Labry to Briey, arriving there at 3:15 p.m. where they spent the next thirty days performing guard and police duty, inspections, and more maneuvers. It is during this time Pvt. Lute Cordova, on December 11th, returned to Company F.

On January 3rd, Amo would have celebrated his twenty-fourth birthday, but for now he is still buried near Magneux, France. January 9th, the 110th is on the move again. Marcelo marches from Briey back through Jarny where they are relieved by the 34th Division, staying in that area until January 18th. The 19th of January the 110th left at 7:30 a.m. and marched east to Conflans for one and a half miles, entrained at Jeandelize and detrain in Barizey-la-Côte. From

Barizey-la-Côte they marched nine miles east to Germiny and were billeted there for the next fifty-eight days, departing March 18th.

However, to the northwest of them, two more casualties. While many were enthusiastic about the prospects of going home, two wealthy volunteers, Dorothea, and Gladys Cromwell, twin sisters from New York, had other thoughts. They had volunteered for the Red Cross near the front at Chalon-sur-Marne where for eight months they pushed their lives to exhaustion in serving humanity. Harriet Rogers, assistant head of the canteen, described the Cromwell twins:

> They are angels who not only do first-class work on day or night service, but also find time to visit soldiers in the French hospitals and to befriend the little French refugee children. Everybody loves them and admires their efficiency and courage in real danger.[65]

According to the Green-Wood blog, in the biographical Note to Gladys's book of poems, published in 1919, their Red Cross work in France is described as follows:

> For eight months they worked under fire on long day and night shifts; their free time was filled with volunteer outside service; they slept in "caves" or under trees in a field; they suffered from the exhaustion that is so acute to those who have never known physical labor; yet no one suspected until the end came that for many months they believed their work a failure, and their efforts futile . . . overwhelming strain and fatigue had made them more weary than they realized, and the horrors of conditions near the Front broke their already overtaxed endurance.[66]

They chose to jump off the ship, SS *La Lorraine*, while leaving port at Bordeaux Harbor, on their scheduled voyage back home to New York. Both are interred at Surennes American Military Cemetery, on a hill overlooking Paris.

On Friday, February 28, 1919, the good news and bad news appeared on the front page of the *Stars and Stripes*. The sailing dates for 28th Division along with some other divisions were posted and it would be in May, but no date was given. Also, on the front page was the headline "Cable is Awaited for Disposition of 70,000 Graves" regarding the assembly and final disposition of America's graves in Europe. Until they would depart, they were kept busy with terrain exercises, divisional horse shows, football games, and more training. Keep em' busy and out of trouble— far from wine, women, and song. Well— a song was okay. Lute Cordova should be in this photo since he re-joins the company in December. Marcelo is in the back row, (see Figure 36) fourth from the left. An uncropped photo can be found on linehttps://www.facebook.com/28ID.AEF.WWI/.

Figure 35. Photo of Company F in Germiny, France

PART III

The Journey Home

Photo # NH 104644   Troops board USS Santa Olivia at St. Nazaire, France

Figure 36. The Journey Home, 28th Division boarding the SS Santa Olivia

Donation of Dr. Mark Kulikowski, 2007; U.S. Naval Historical Center Photograph

★

CHAPTER 16

Marcelo comes Home

On March 9ᵗʰ, they started preparing to leave for Le Mans, over 250 miles west of Germiny, France. Finally— they were on the move, leaving Germiny at 12:15 p.m., marching back to Barizey-la-Côte, arriving at 3:20 p.m., and departing at 5:15 p.m. via train.

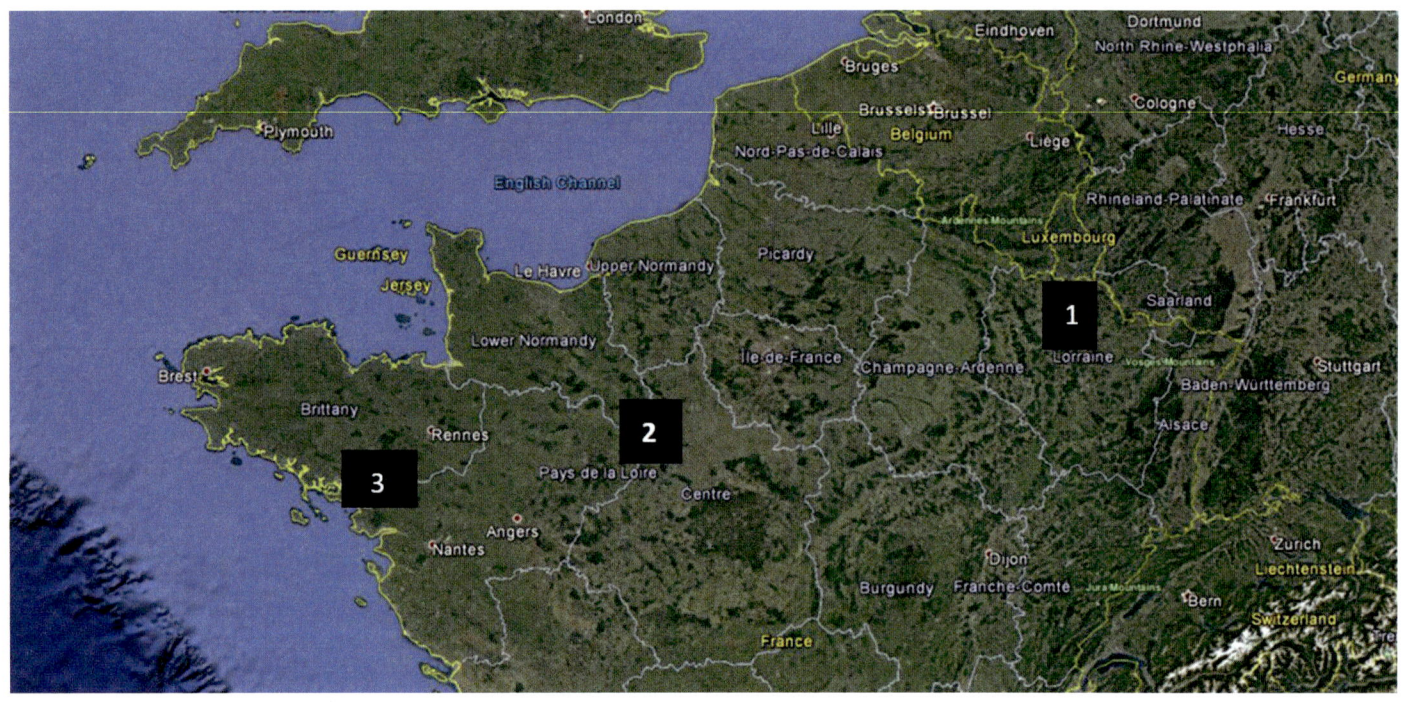

Figure 37. En route to Saint-Nazaire port

1. Lorraine Region: November – March 20ᵗʰ

2. Le Mans: March 21ˢᵗ – Apr 18ᵗʰ

3. Saint-Nazaire: April 19ᵗʰ – 29ᵗʰ

Photo # NH 104640   USS Santa Olivia at St. Nazaire, France

SS Santa Olivia at Saint-Nazaire, France

Photo # NH 104645   French Army band plays for troops boarding USS Santa Olivia, 30 May 1919

Figure 38. A French band for the homeward bound troops

Photo # NH 104642   USS Santa Olivia leaving St. Nazaire, France

Figure 39. SS Santa Olivia leaving Saint-Nazaire, France

Donation of Dr. Mark Kulikowski, 2007; U.S. Naval Historical Center

Marcelo, Lute, and the Second Battalion arrived March 21st in Le Mans at two-thirty in the morning, after two days and nine hours; they had lost six hours due to a train wreck. They would be in a Forwarding Camp, Le Mans, for twenty-eight days, where they engaged in work and training as per Camp Regulations and Division Training Schedule. Once again, they were informed to prepare to leave April 18th. They marched from the Forwarding Camp to the railroad yards at Le Mans and entrained for Saint Nazaire at 8:40 p.m., another ten-hour train ride in the right direction.

They arrived at St. Nazaire at 7:30 a.m. and marched to Camp No. 2 where they were once again inspected, and then advanced to Camp No. 1. Here they would spend the next ten days, preparing for embarkation, regimental reviews, and general inspections. Then on

April 29th, Marcelo, the Second Battalion, Third Battalion, and enlisted men from Companies M and E marched from the Embarkation Camp at 11:50 a.m. to Pier No. 6. There they embarked on the SS *Santa Olivia* and sailed at 4 p.m. Not yet a movie star, coxswain Humphrey Bogart who was assigned to this ship may have been on board serving his time in the Navy.

Photo # NH 104641   USS Santa Olivia leaving St Nazaire, France

Figure 40. SS Santa Olivia leaving the port of Saint-Nazaire, France

Donation of Dr. Mark Kulikowski, 2007; U.S. Naval Historical Center Photograph

One more stop before their voyage on the high seas, they would travel north, along the coast to Brest for oil and leave the next day at 11:00 a.m. Privates Marcelo, Lute, and others of the 110th Regiment were traveling approximately 300 miles a day; they would arrive in Philadelphia on May 12th, 4 p.m., a twelve-day journey.

Figure 41. Marcelo arrives in Philadelphia, Pa. May 12, 1919

Photo from the History of the 110th Association

ALONG THE PARADE AT PHILADELPHIA, PA., MAY 15, 1919.

(Courtesy Army & Navy Journal)

Figure 42. Marcelo and Lute in a Philadelphia parade.

Photo from the History of the 110th Association

Another ship arrived the evening before at 8 p.m., but it may not have had the fanfare that greeted the SS *Santa Olivia* when it appeared. There they debarked and took a train, a thirty-two-mile trip to Camp Dix, New Jersey. The next day, they were under Regiment review again, but on the 15th they headed back to Philadelphia to be in a parade and returned to Camp Dix. On Friday, May 23rd, the entire 110th Regiment of 55th Brigade was mustered out. Privates Marcelo and Lute were no longer in the military, no more reviews. Now, back to Huerfano County, another 1,700-mile train ride at 5 cents a mile from the place of discharge to his actual bona fide home or residence. In Marcelo and Lute's case, it would be about 85.00 dollars or over 1,200 dollars in May of 2019.

Unfortunately, or fortunately, Marcelo most likely missed the Stag Party given Thursday evening, May 29th, to welcome troops home. It was sponsored by the Red Cross Chapter of Huerfano County and assisted by the Elks Club. Since the affair is "stag" "throughout, the local Elks will have charge of the entertainment. Wide publicity is desired so that every veteran of the late war of the Spanish-American War, and of the Civil war, may be on hand to enjoy the occasion." Walsenburg World, Vol XXX, No. 20, May 22, 1919

CHAPTER 17

Amo comes Home

April is the cruellest month, breeding Lilacs out of the dead land, mixing Memory and desire, stirring Dull roots with spring rain . . . ."

— T.S. Eliot

While Marcelo and the 110th were in the Lorraine Region of France, in the winter and spring of 1919, life was stirring again on last year's battlefields. This time it was the Graves Registration Service, a division of the Quartermasters Corps. The War Department had announced in the *Stars and Stripes* that Congress will finally provide for the return of all bodies desired returned, but that at least half of our dead, by the preference of those concerned, will rest permanently in France. As of February 28th, no dead had been returned to the United States. On February 28th, 1919 The *Stars and Stripes* went on to say the following, under the heading of Cable is awaited for Disposition of 70,000 Graves:

> . . . In the meantime, the AEF is gathering its dead together, that in death they may be as they were in life—in serried ranks, shoulder to shoulder, comrades. From frozen dugouts, from old ruins, from those hastily improvised and now sunken openings in the ground that were shell holes and battle graves, from wheat field and river bank and meadow knoll, from all for the thousands of places of isolation and great loneliness, the dead are being tenderly lifted and borne to take their places in the ordered ranks of the Army . . .

When Amo was shelled, he was buried immediately near where he was killed, a hastily improvised grave. Company F was in the front line, and the enemy knew when soldiers were assembling, and would shell that area again. Fellow soldiers would quickly gather the remains and bury him as soon as possible. The following is an excerpt from Chaplain Charles Schall of the 110th Regiment, titled "Our Heroic Dead"

The method of burial on the fighting front was to wrap the body in a blanket and carefully mark the place of the grave. To guard against any mistake one of the two metal identification disks, which every soldier wore, was securely fastened on the remains and the other nailed to the wooden marker always placed at the head of the grave. In addition, a paper on which the name, number date of death, cause of death and date of burial were written in hard pencil, was tacked to the marker and another paper on which the same facts were written was placed in a bottle and buried neck downward at the foot of the grave with just enough covering to protect it from the weather.

Before the act of burial, a man's pockets were searched for any personal effects. These carefully wrapped and labeled were turned over to the Supply Officer of the Regiment who in turn delivered them to the Division Quartermaster's office. The plan contemplated the ultimate arrival of these effects at the Effects Bureau, Hoboken, New Jersey, from which point they were to be sent to the nearest relatives.[67]

It was probably in March 1919, that the bodies of Amo, Moses, Joyce Kilmer, and other soldiers killed between the Meuse and the Vesle in 1918 were retrieved. Moses and Joyce Kilmer were interred in the Oise-Aisne American Cemetery. Theodore Roosevelt requested that his son Quentin lie where he fell. Quentin would remain in Chamery until 1955 when he is reburied in Normandy, next to his older brother, Theodore Jr., who died in World War II. Many soldiers were buried by churches, and the U.S. Graves troops found that they had been well taken care of by the French. Many women adopted the fallen, decorating the graves with flowers as if they were their children.[68]

By April 4th many families had the choice of either leaving their sons in France or bringing them back to America. Sgt. Joyce Kilmer, Alan Seeger, and Pvt. Moses Benavidez are all buried in France, where approximately 30 percent of families chose overseas burial. Amo's parents decided to bring Amo back to Huerfano County. It would not be until Sunday, March 19, 1922, that Amo and many others were shipped on the SS *Cambria*, from the Port of Antwerp, Belgium. From there they would sail to Brooklyn, New York, scheduled to arrive on Wednesday, March 29th. It would be another twenty-three days before his body reached Walsenburg.

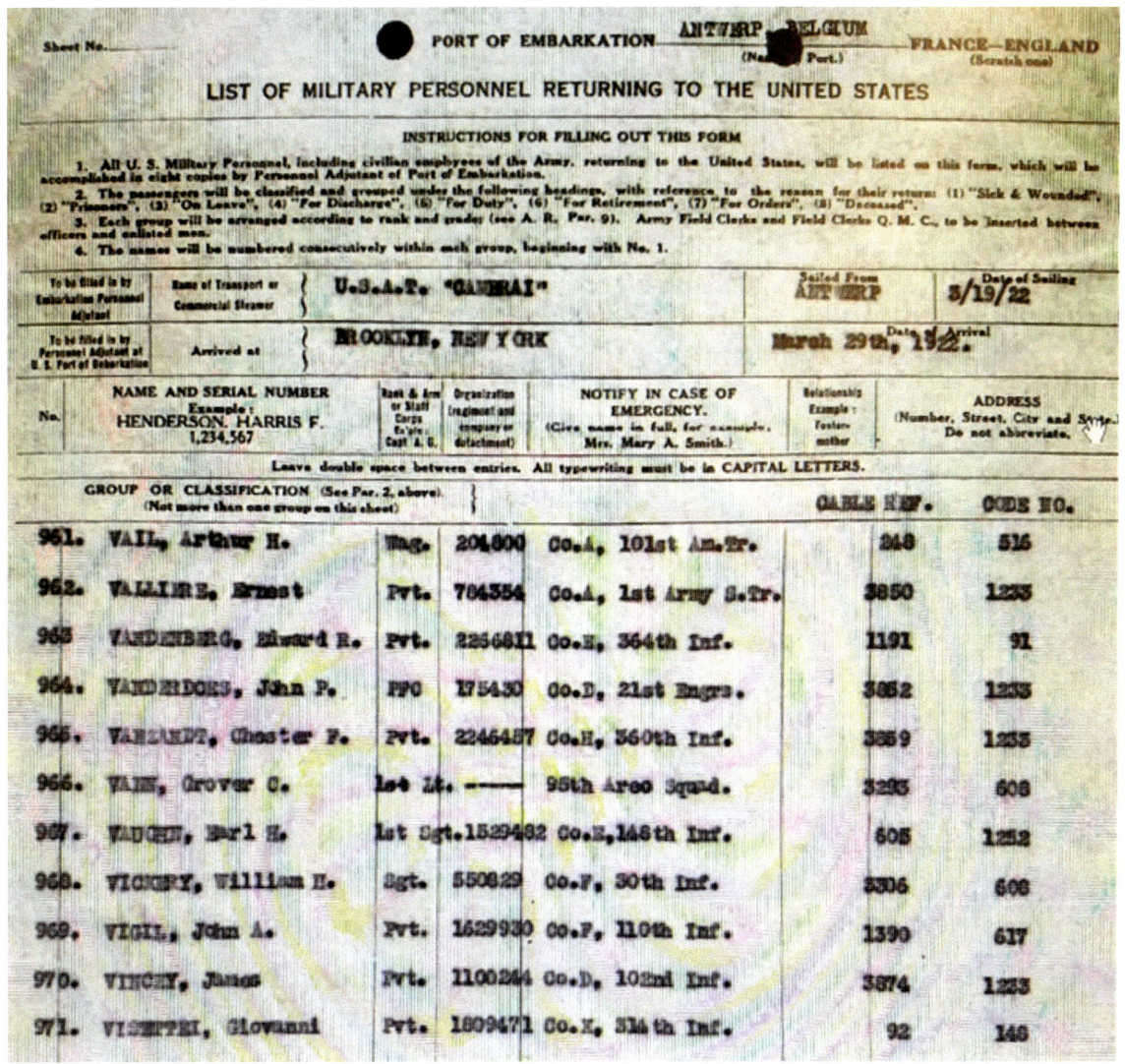

Figure 43. Amo on the SS Cambrai, Antwerp, Belgium to Brooklyn, New York

Figure 44. Military Funeral for Deceased Soldier, The Walsenburg World, 1922

In the *Walsenburg World*, Tuesday, April 18th, two days after Easter Sunday, Amo made the front page again, announcing his return scheduled for Thursday, 6:20 p.m. Awaiting Amo that day was a military escort of the American Legion and most likely his family. If Marcelo were there, it would have been three years and seven months since his last day with Amo. Now Marcelo would have to tell the story of how Amo died all over again, even if people knew it. Amo was taken to his parents North Veta home, overlooking the Cucharas River. It was where his grandparents had homesteaded over fifty years ago.

CHAPTER 18

A Solemn Huerfano County Salute

On Sunday morning, a small ceremony was held at the Vigil residence (see Fig.1) in North Veta. Then the American Legion escorted Amo back to Walsenburg, for a 2 p.m. ceremony at the County Courthouse. The Marshall brass band furnished the music, and Rev. F. M. Spence of Pueblo addressed the afternoon Sunday gathering. According to the *Walsenburg World*, Amo was the last of the Huerfano County citizen soldiers of World War One to be buried in Huerfano County. Charles F. Elmire of Redwing was buried the day before in Gardner, and Anastacio Trujillo, one of the brave Forty-Four was buried Saturday in the south Catholic cemetery. The County was very supportive in demonstrating its appreciation for these men making the supreme sacrifice.

Amo was buried in the Masonic Cemetery Vigil family plot near his grandparents Juan D. and Monulita Valdez-Vigil, Sunday afternoon, April 23rd. He would not get a military upright headstone until his brother-law, forty-eight-year-old Claud T. Swift, entering his sixth year as sheriff applied for a headstone in April 1940. It was shipped May 24, 1940, just in time for Memorial Day 1940.

Marcelo came home to his young wife Sara and raised a family in the Pass Creek area; family members still reside in Huerfano County.[69] They would live and work in Huerfano County, Denver, and other places, but Huerfano County was home. On Tuesday, June 3, 1986, ninety-one-year-old Marcelo was laid to rest at the Masonic Cemetery, less than ninety yards from Amo.

Notes

Epigraph

1. Mastriano, Alvin York, 191.

Preface

2. Association of the 110th, 285.
3. Ibid. 265.
4. The Independent, The Forty and Four Braves, October 5, 1917, 1.
5. Association of the 110th, 58.
6. Darryl Cordova, grandson of Marcelo Reynolds.
7. McCullough, Truman, 102.
8. Remarque, All Quiet on the Western Front, iv.

Acknowledgements

9. Darryl Cordova, grandson of Marcelo Reynolds.
10. Haas, Army History Spring 2017, Book Reviews. 44-45.

Introduction

11. Wikipedia, World War I casualties.
12. CDC, 1918 Pandemic (H1N1 virus), https://www.cdc.gov/flu/pandemic-resources/1918-pandemic-h1n1.html.
13. Gibbs, Realities of War, 363.
14. Ferguson, The Pity of War, xxiv.
15. Psalms 2:1, New American Standard Bible.
16. Ree, Walsenburg- Crossroads, 81.
17. Ibid. 77.
18. The Independent, Forty Huerfano Soldiers to Leave Next Wednesday, September 28, 1917, 1.
19. Sides, Blood and Thunder, 71.
20. Bernet, *314 Motor Supply Train,* 23.

Part I: Over Here

Chapter 1 Consider the Years of Many Generations

21. Christofferson, Lost Communities of Huerfano: North Veta. World Journal Huerfano. January 19, 2012.

22. World-Independent, 1945. Damaso [*sic*] Vigil Sr., County Pioneer Dies Wednesday. December 20.

23. American Battle Monuments Commission, 15-16.

24. Eric B. Setzekorn (Setzekorn 2017), Joining the Great War April 1917-April 1918, 16.

Chapter 2 War Now On!

Chapter 3 Extra Extra, First Call

Chapter 4 We're Coming Lafayette

25. Denver and Rio Grande-Western Pacific, Colorado and New Mexico Lines, July-August 1917.

26. Setzekorn, Joining the Great War, 24.

27. Bernet, *314 Motor Supply Train*, 11.

Chapter 5 Back to the Old World

28. Ibid. 25.

29. Walsenburg World. 1918. Herbert Harmes in Battle. October 17: 5.

30. Baker, Doughboy's Diary, 14.

31. Bernet, 314 Motor Supply Train, 23.

Chapter 6 Camp Disagreeable

32. Army History, Glad I was in it, Spring 2017, 10.

33. Association of the 110th 43.

Part II: We are here Lafayette

Chapter 7 The Land of the Crushed Grape

34. Ibid., 58.

35. Ibid., 285.

36. Ibid., 265.

37. Ibid., 199.

38. Ibid., 185.

39. Ibid., 285.

40. Ibid., 283.

41. Ibid., 239.

42. Ibid., 146.

43. Wawro, Sons of Freedom, 20.

Chapter 8 The Second Battle of the Marne

Chapter 9 On the trail of the Hun

44. Association of the 110th 58.

45. Walsenburg World. 1918. Herbert Harmes in Battle. October 17: 5.

46. Ohl, The Keystone Division in the Great War.94.

47. Association of the 110th 185.

48. Lutz, The 110th Infantry in the World War, 38.

Chapter 10 Tree, Bois de Grimpettes

49. Association of the 110th 146.

Chapter 11 Rendezvous with Death

50. Lutz, The 110th Infantry in the World War, 42.

51. Association of the 110th, 74.

Chapter 12 The Runner

52. Army History, Glad I was in it, Spring 2017, 10.

53. NASB, 1 Samuel 4:12.

54. Association of the 110th 165.

55. Ibid., 285.

56. Ibid., 199.

Chapter 13 Moving and Marching

57. Stallings, The Doughboys, 227.

Chapter 14 Fourteen Days in October

58. Armor, The 304th Tank Brigade, July-August 1988, 33.

59. Lutz, The 110th Infantry in the World War, 58.

60. Ibid., 62.

61. History of 328th, 82d Division, 45.

62. York, The Diary of Alvin C. York, https://acacia.pairsite.com/Acacia.Vignettes/The.Diary.of.Alvin.York. html#October%208th%201918.

63. Ibid.

64. Wawro, Sons of Freedom, 369.

Chapter 15 The Thiaucourt Sector

65. Richman, A Twin Tragedy, https://www.green-wood.com/2017/a-twin-tragedy/.

66. Ibid.

Chapter 16 Marcelo comes Home

Chapter 17 Amo comes Home

67. Association of the 110th, 141.

68. Stars and Stripes, The Adopted Graves, June 13, 1919, 4.

Chapter 18 A Solemn Huerfano County Salute

69. Madelyn Cisneros-Sena, granddaughter of Marcelo Reynolds, interview with author, 2018.

Selected Bibliography

2019. *1918 Pandemic (H1N1 virus).* U.S. Department of Health and Human Services. Accessed 2019. https://www.cdc.gov/flu/pandemic-resources/1918-pandemic-h1n1.html.

Baker, Chester E. 1998. *Dougboy's Diary.* Shippensburg: Burd Street Press.

Bernet, Milton E. 1919. *The Three Hundred and Fourteenth Motor Supply Train in the World War.* St. Louis. Accessed 2018. https://babel.hathitrust.org/cgi/pt?id=loc.ark:/13960/t1jh42537;view=1up;seq=1.

Christofferson, Nancy. 2012. "Lost Communities of Huerfano: North Veta." *World Journal Huerfano.* Electronic and Print. Walsenburg, Colorado, January 19. https://huerfanoworldjournal.com/lost-communities-of-huerfano-north-veta/.

Cordova, Darryl, interview by Carl P Lucero. 2017. *Marcelo Reynolds* North Veta, Colorado.

Ferguson, Niall. 1998. *The Pity of War.* Basic Books.

Gibbs, Philip Armand Hamiliton. 1920. *Realities of War.* Prod. Internet Archive. London. https://archive.org/details/realitiesofwar00gibbuoft/page/n1.

Haas, Darrin. Spring 2017. "Doughboys on the Great War." *Army History*, 56. Accessed 2018. https://history.army.mil/armyhistory/AH103(W).pdf.

Herring Jr., George C. 2017. "Glad I Was in it An Iowa Doughboy in the Great War, 1918-1919." *Army History*, Spring ed.: 55.

1920. *History of Three Hundred and Twenty-Eight Infantry Eight-Second Division, A.E.F.* Electronic. Accessed 2018. https://archive.org/details/historyofthreehu00slsn.

Infantry, Association of the 110th. n.d. "History of the 110th Infantry (10th Pa.) of the 28th Division, U.S.A., 1917-1919: a compilation of orders, citations, maps, records, and illustrations relating to the 3rd Pa. Inf., 10th Pa.

Inf., and 110th U.S. Inf." *History of the 110th Infantry Pennsylvania.* Internet Archive; Print. Prod. University of Pittsburgh Library System. Pittsburgh. https://archive.org/stream/historyof110thin00asso#mode/2up.

Kelly, John F. 2016. *U.S. Department of Defense.* January 8. Accessed 2018. https://dod.defense.gov/News/Transcripts/Transcript-View/Article/642104/department-of-defense-press-briefing-by-general-kelly-in-the-pentagon-briefing/.

Lutz, Francis Earle. 1919. *The 110th Infantry.* Haddonfield, New Jersey. https://books.google.com/books?id=TZT-GAAAAMAAJ&pg=PA13&lpg=PA13&dq=Francis+E+Lutz&source=bl&ots=572LlbYEhD&sig=ACfU3U2ucx-DyvICeREX25fwBF15c4.

Mastriano, Douglas V. 2014. *Alvin York: A New Biography of the Hero of the Argonne.* Lexington, Ky: University Press of Kentucky.

Ohl, John Kennedy. 1978. *The Keystone Division in the Great War.* https://www.mesacc.edu/static/social-science/The%20Keystone%20Division%20in%20the%20Great%20War.pdf.

Ree, Dorothy Rose. 2006. *Walsenburg-Crossroads Town.* Walsenburg, Colorado: Nocturn Independent Publishing.

Richman, Jeff. 2017. *A Twin Tragedy.* Green-Wood Historian Blog. January 23. https://www.green-wood.com/2017/a-twin-tragedy/.

Rogge, Robert E. 1988. "The 304th Tank Brigade." *Amor*, July - August: 56.

Setzekorn, Eric B. 2017. "U.S. Army Campaigns of World War I: Joining the Great War, April 1917- April 1918." *U.S. Army Campaigns of World War I Series.* Defense Department, Army, Center of Military History. Washington, D.C., March 3. https://history.army.mil/catalog/pubs/77/77-2.html.

Stallings, Lawrence. 1963. *The Doughboys, The Story of The AEF, 1917-1918.* New York, Evanston, and London: Harper & Row, Publishers.

The Independent. 1917. "Forty-Four Brave Soldier Reception." October 6.

The Walsenburg World. 1918. "Herbert Harmes in Battle." October 17: 8. https://www.coloradohistoricnewspapers.org/?a=d&d=WWWI9181017-01&e=-------en-20--1--txt-txIN.

Wawro, Geoffrey. 2018. *Sons of Freedom The Forgotten American Soldiers who Defeated Germany in World War I*. New York: Basic Books.

World-Independent. 1945. "Damaso [*sic*] Vigil Sr., County Pioneer Dies Wednesday." December 20.

Yank, A. 1919. "The Adopted Graves." *The Stars and Stripes*, June 13: 4. Accessed 2018. https://www.loc.gov/resource/20001931/1919-06-13/ed-1/?sp=4&q=%22The+Adopted+Graves%22&r=0.114,-0.039,0.786,0.383,0.